EXECUTE FIRST

EXECUTE FIRST
STOP PREPAIRING, START ACHIEVING

The Execution System Behind
Billion Dollar Businesses & Elite Performers

RYAN GRIMES

HENSLEY
PRESS

EXECUTE FIRST
Stop Preparing, Start Achieving
First Printing, 2026
ISBN 979-8-9954942-1-8 Paperback
     979-8-9954942-2-5 Ebook

DEDICATION

This book is for my incredible daughter, Hensley. You are my single biggest achievement and the truest source of my pride and motivation. I love you more than life itself.

To my Grandparents, my unwavering rocks, my constants and the foundation of my life. You are the reason I am who I am today.

To Sarah, who for the past 10 years has always believed in me and supported my craziest endeavors. Your love and companionship has allowed me to pursue and realize my dreams.

To my friends:

Jon, for your consistent presence, your words of advice and your friendship.

Ian, for our intellectual conversations, your relentless motivation and constant encouragement for me to be better.

To the Marine Corps, for instilling in me the power of perseverance and the ability to overcome any adversity.

And to all others who have walked in and out of my life, your influence, however long or brief, has contributed to my journey and the pages within this book.

CONTENTS

INTRODUCTION

Seeing the college seal on the envelope made me sick to my stomach. I opened the letter, and two words jumped off the page and eternally etched themselves into my memory:

"Academic suspension."

Two and a half years of half-assed effort, missed classes, and last-minute panic had led to this single, devastating, and life-changing moment. My "plans" had just disintegrated into thin air. No more transferring to Texas Tech to study Architecture. No more relationship with my high school sweetheart, who had counted on me joining her at Texas Tech (she was already there). No more college at all.

THE NEXT AFTERNOON

The day after I received the letter, I was driving home from campus for what would be my final time. My old truck rumbled beneath me, and the engine noise mirrored the churning in my stomach. Frustrated, I gripped the steering wheel so tight my knuckles turned white.

I wasn't thinking about my future. I wasn't thinking about what would come next. I just kept replaying the same question over and over:

"*What in the hell am I supposed to do now?*"

I had disappointed my grandparents, who'd been nothing but encouraging and supportive. I had let down my girlfriend, who had been waiting for me to get my act together. I had just proven every doubt I'd ever had about myself.

I was a failure. Not because I lacked talent. Not because I wasn't smart enough. But because I didn't do what I knew I needed to do. I couldn't consistently make myself do the work that mattered, regardless of whether I wanted to do it.

The light ahead turned red. I stopped at the intersection, still gripping that steering wheel, still drowning in that question: "*What in the hell am I supposed to do now?*"

Then I saw it. Across the intersection, tucked into a tired strip mall between a dry cleaner and a check-cashing place, there was a small sign I'd driven past a thousand times without ever noticing.

"U.S. Marine Corps Recruiter."

As soon as I noticed it, my grandfather's voice echoed in my mind. He was a retired Air Force Master Sergeant, and for as long as I could remember, he had been urging me to join the military. Never forcefully. Just as a quiet suggestion:

"You know Ryan, you should join the service. It would be good for you."

I had dismissed it every single time without any hesitation. In fact, the thought had never crossed my mind, not even for a millisecond. The military wasn't part of my plan. Architecture was the plan. Success was the plan. The military was for people who had no other options. But sitting at that red light, staring at academic suspension with no plan B, I realized something:

I didn't have better options.

The light turned green.

THE DECISION

I pressed the gas.

No hesitation. No internal debate about pros and cons. No weighing of options or considering alternatives. I drove through the intersection, turned right, and pulled into the parking lot.

When I parked, I wasn't thinking about my future. I wasn't thinking about redemption or purpose, or becoming a better version of myself. I was only thinking one thing:

"Do something."

I walked across the parking lot, pushed open the glass door, and found a single uniformed Marine sitting at his desk. He looked up as I entered, stood up, and asked:

"What can I do for you?"

Without hesitation, I heard myself speak words that didn't even feel like my own:

"What do I have to do to become a Marine?"

WHAT CHANGED

There was no inspirational music swelling in the background. Just a seemingly spontaneous decision made at a red light. And it changed everything for me.

Not because I suddenly had perfect clarity about my future.

I didn't.

Not because some motivational lightning bolt struck me.

It didn't.

And definitely not because I felt confident or prepared.

I was far from it.

It changed everything because that single decision began to reveal a pattern I would spend the next 25 years of my life researching, understanding, and leveraging.

That moment at the red light wasn't just about action.

It was about executing before I had clarity (the clarity wouldn't come until much later).

It was about choosing a new identity (I would become a Marine before I felt like one).

It was about committing to discipline (boot camp would force that, at first).

It was about deciding quickly (no analysis paralysis, just execution).

It was about trusting the process (I had no idea if it would work).

One decision. Five core principles. All working together.

THIRTEEN WEEKS LATER

Thirteen weeks after walking into that recruiting office, I stood in formation on the parade deck at Marine Corps Recruit Depot San Diego, wearing dress blues for the first time as a United States Marine.

I had graduated from boot camp and become a United States Marine.

I was leaner, harder and more focused than I'd ever been in my life. For the first time, I understood what discipline and purpose actually felt like, not because someone told me about them, but because I had lived them.

But those thirteen weeks between the recruiting office and graduation weren't some motivational movie montage of brief moments of discomfort. They were relentlessly brutal. They were physically miserable and painful. They were emotionally difficult. I felt genuine fear and doubted my own capabilities. I questioned my own beliefs.

When I stood in formation on that parade deck, I wasn't the same person who had walked into that recruiting office thirteen weeks earlier. Not because boot camp had given me some mystical transformation. But because I had proven to myself that I could do hard things that I never believed I was capable of doing. That I could execute first without knowing the outcome. That I could be the person I wanted to become before I had become that person. That I could make myself do what needed to be done, consistently, regardless of how I felt. That I could take decisive action and pivot quickly. That I could trust the process even though I couldn't see the progress I was making.

That academic suspension letter represented a version of me who knew what to do but couldn't make himself do it. The Marine standing on that parade deck was a version of me who had learned the opposite: execution beats intention, every time.

WHAT I ACTUALLY LEARNED

People assume the Marine Corps teaches you to be tough. It does, but that's not the most valuable thing I learned. People assume it teaches you discipline. It does, but that wasn't my core insight either. The most valuable thing I learned while serving in the Marine Corps was this: The people who succeed in achieving their goals execute through universal principles that work as a complete system. This concept was never taught to me in a classroom. It was just embedded in every aspect of Marine Corps culture. It was how we lived. They were mantras we barked at each other.

"Bias for Action" meant: executing on incomplete information and that being wrong was almost always preferable to waiting for complete information and doing nothing.

"Every Marine a rifleman" meant: identity is what drives your results.

"Suck it up" meant: discipline always beats motivation.

"Semper Gumby" meant: always be ready and willing to pivot.

"The more you sweat in peace, the less you bleed in war" meant trust the work will work for you.

After serving five years in the Marines and nearly 20 years building and leading businesses, coaching leaders and entrepreneurs, reading biographies, and having countless conversations with people across a wide array of industries, I kept seeing the same pattern. And I kept asking the same question:

"What separates people who achieve their goals from people who don't?"

These people who achieved their goals weren't exceptional people with unique advantages. They were just ordinary people applying extraordinary principles.

The same principles I had indirectly learned as a Marine. The same principles I had used to build numerous businesses. The same principles that separate achievers from dreamers across every field and discipline.

Over the next 20 years, I became obsessed with understanding why some people execute and others don't.

The same five universal principles emerged every time:

Principle 1: Action Creates Clarity. You don't think your way to clarity. You move your way to it. The path reveals itself to those who walk it, not those who study the maps.

Principle 2: Identity Drives Results. You don't achieve outcomes and then become someone new. You become someone new first, and outcomes follow. Every action is a credit for who you are becoming.

Principle 3: Discipline Beats Motivation. Motivation is a feeling. Discipline is a structure. Feelings fluctuate. Structures persist. You build systems that run regardless of how you feel.

Principle 4: Decide Fast, Adjust Faster. Speed beats perfection. Learning beats analysis. You decide with 70% of the information you wish you had, execute immediately, and adjust based on real-life feedback.

Principle 5: Trust The Invisible Work. Breakthrough happens after long, difficult, invisible phases, not instead of them. Your results always lag, while the work you put in compounds over time. You track inputs, trust the process, and persist when everyone else quits.

One word in that system deserves clarity before we go any further. Throughout this book, I use the word *"execution"* deliberately, not *"action."* Action is any movement. Execution is deliberate, intentional movement driven by a system and aimed at a specific outcome. When I ask you to execute, I am not asking you to move randomly. I'm asking you to move with purpose, with a defined question you're trying to answer, and with the intention to extract a lesson from whatever happens next. That distinction runs through every principle in this book.

These aren't five separate ideas. They are a single integrated execution system where each principle feeds the next. Action generates clarity. Clarity shapes identity. Identity drives discipline. Discipline enables speed. Speed produces more action. All while invisible work compounds underground until the breakthrough arrives.

These aren't tactics. They *aren't* industry-specific strategies. They are universal laws of execution that govern achievement across every field. That's the Execute First system. And that's what this book teaches you.

THE BOOK YOU'RE HOLDING

This book exists only because I applied these five principles.

I had been thinking about writing this book for years before I actually started. I had accumulated countless pages of notes I had jotted down here and there, dozens of case studies, and I had a very rough outline, if you could even call it that. But I had never written a book, so I had no idea where to even begin.

One morning, staring at a blinking cursor on a blank computer screen, I made the same decision I'd made at that stoplight 25 years earlier:

Execute.

I didn't feel ready. I wasn't entirely sure what the book would look like. I didn't have a perfect outline. Hell, I didn't even know if anyone would want to read it. I just started writing. Some mornings, I wrote 1,500 words and felt like I was channeling something greater than myself. Most mornings, I wrote 400 to 600 words, and it felt like I was fighting a losing battle. A few mornings, I barely scraped together 200 words. But I wrote something every morning at 5:30

AM. No exceptions. The book has been through countless revisions. It grew, shrank, and changed direction more times than I can count.

I didn't write this book from the mountaintop. I wrote it from the trenches. And that's exactly where the principles matter most. Because anyone can execute when conditions are perfect, the question is: can you execute when conditions *aren't* perfect? When you *don't* feel ready. When you *don't* have proof it will work. When results *aren't* visible yet. That's when the five principles separate people who achieve from people who only daydream about it.

YOUR STOPLIGHT MOMENT

Right now, you're exactly where I was when I was sitting in my truck 25 years ago.

You know you're capable of more. You know you've been waiting too long. You recognize the gap between where you currently are and where you want to be. The only question is: Will you execute?

Not "when you're ready." Not "after one more book." Not "when conditions are perfect." Right now.

Ready is a myth. These five principles are real, and they're universal.

Your light is green.

SECTION 1
THE FUNDAMENTALS

1. EXECUTION BEATS PERFECT PREPARATION

"The secret to getting ahead is getting started." - Mark Twain

In 2009, an unemployed Ukrainian immigrant named Jan Koum began developing an app that Facebook would buy for $19 billion only 5 years later. That app was WhatsApp.

There was no master plan. No perfect preparation. No moment when Jan felt ready. There was just execution.

Across Silicon Valley, around the same time he was creating WhatsApp, another social app was being developed by a better-funded, better-staffed, better-prepared company. They raised $41 million before launching anything. They hired 38 engineers. They rented a huge 22,000-square-foot office in Palo Alto with beanbag chairs and even had a half-pipe skateboard ramp. They had everything they needed and more, but three years later, they were gone.

THE TWO APPROACHES

In early 2009, Jan Koum was 33 years old, jobless, and watching his savings disappear. In 2007, he was rejected by both Facebook and Twitter despite having spent nearly a decade at Yahoo. He had no business plan, no funding, and no team. What he did have was a $99 iPhone developer account, his friend Brian Acton, whom he'd met at Yahoo, and one idea: a simple status update app that let people communicate without paying the expensive text message fees phone companies charged at the time. He didn't wait until the idea was fully formed. He just started building it.

A tech veteran named Bill Nguyen was building the other app. Nguyen was a serial entrepreneur with previous exits to Apple and Phone.com worth hundreds of millions of dollars. He had connections, credentials, and credibility that Jan Koum couldn't have even dreamt of having.

In 2010, he co-founded Color Labs with Peter Pham. Their goal was to create a revolutionary photo-sharing app that would create "elastic networks." Based on the user's location, it would allow them to see photos taken by nearby strangers without usernames or passwords. The vision was bold, and their preparation was meticulous. Between 2010 and 2011, before Color Labs had launched anything or acquired a single user, they had raised $25 million from Sequoia Capital, $9 million from Bain Capital, and $7 million in venture debt from Silicon Valley Bank. They spent $350,000 to purchase the domain Color.com. Everything was *perfect*, and everything was *ready*.

THE BROKEN LAUNCH

After about 6 months of developing WhatsApp, just weeks after it launched, Jan sat in his apartment staring at crash logs on his aging MacBook. The app had gone down twelve times in an hour, and his handful of early users were leaving one-star reviews in the App Store. They called it the worst messaging app ever. One wrote that it crashed every time he opened it. Another told anyone reading not to waste their time. While most people would have seen those reviews and quit, Jan dove into the code.

Four hours later, he found it: a memory leak in the message queue. Every time a user received multiple messages in quick succession, the app's memory would overflow and crash. He fixed it, pushed the update to Apple's servers, and went to bed. By morning, crash reports had dropped by nearly 80 percent.

That single debugging session taught Jan more about what users actually needed than six months of market research would have. Not because the crash was instructive in theory, but because real users were hitting a real problem in a real product. That revealed something no survey ever could: they didn't want features, they just wanted the app to work.

THE PERFECT LAUNCH

On March 24, 2011, Color Labs launched to a tech world watching with great anticipation. Forty-one million dollars in funding, Bill Nguyen's track record, and months of meticulous high-level development. Everyone expected something remarkable.

Users were immediately confused by the app's core functionality. Creating location-based photo networks with strangers wasn't intuitive. It required a critical mass of nearby users to work properly, and at launch, the user base was too small and too dispersed to create the dynamic networks Color had promised. One reviewer captured it plainly: "It would be pointless even if I managed to understand how it works." The initial App Store rating was only two out of five stars.

THE PIVOT

Within weeks of WhatsApp's launch, something unexpected happened. Users weren't using the app the way Jan had designed it. He had built it as a status update tool, but users were treating it like a text messaging platform, typing messages back and forth in the status field itself. They had essentially hacked his app to do something it wasn't designed for. Jan had two choices: defend his original vision or follow the user behavior.

He chose the latter and rebuilt WhatsApp as a messaging platform. Every feature decision from that point forward was based on watching what users actually did in the app. He saw that users wanted simplicity, so he removed features rather than adding them. Users wanted reliability, so he focused on up-time rather than animations. Users wanted privacy, so he added encryption before it was trendy.

Meanwhile, Color Labs had built exactly what they envisioned. The problem was that users didn't want what the company envisioned. Within weeks of launch, co-founder Bill Nguyen admitted in an interview: "We threw out a network you don't know how to get good at. We threw a mountain at people." Co-founder Peter Pham left the company in June 2011, just three months after the launch. By September 2011, six months after launch, Color had fewer than 100,000 active users despite having one million downloads. They attempted multiple pivots, such as live video broadcasting and a partnership with Verizon. Nothing gained traction.

THE OUTCOME

October 2012: Color Labs shut down. Apple acquired the engineering team in an acqui-hire for approximately $7 million. Forty-one million invested. Seven million returned. A loss of $34 million.

On February 19, 2014, Facebook acquired WhatsApp for $19 billion. Nineteen. **Billion**. Dollars.

Same opportunity. Similar timing. Two completely different approaches. Totally opposite outcomes.

WHAT NOBODY SAW

Here's what's easy to miss about that $19 billion outcome: it didn't look like success for most of the journey.

By 2011, WhatsApp was handling one billion messages per day. Impressive, but invisible to most of the world. Facebook and Twitter dominated headlines while WhatsApp grew quietly. No press releases. No flashy marketing campaigns. Just steady, unglamorous growth driven by one thing: it worked, and people told other people it worked.

By 2013, WhatsApp had 200 million active users. Still, most investors dismissed it, saying things like: "It's just a messaging app," and "There's no business model." Jan kept building anyway.

Five years of work that looked like nothing from the outside. Five years of compounding iterations, each one building on the last, none of them individually dramatic enough to make headlines. That's not an accident or a footnote, it's the mechanism. The outcome at the end of those five years wasn't despite the work nobody noticed. It was precisely because of it. That mechanism, invisible work compounding over time, is the subject of Chapter 10. For now, what I want you to focus on is this: Jan didn't outperform Color Labs because he had a better vision, had a better plan, or was more prepared. He outperformed them because he stayed in motion even when there was no external evidence that it would pay off.

This matters for you because the gap between where you are and where you want to be will also look invisible for most of the journey. More importantly, you won't be able to see the path in front of you until you begin heading down it.

So how does this happen? How does a person with no funding, no team, and no complete vision outperform a well-funded, well-staffed, meticulously prepared competitor, and how can you replicate it in your own life? I'll answer these questions, and more, but first, you need to understand something:

Imperfect execution beats perfect preparation, and waiting has a cost you cannot recover.

THE THREE LIES OF READINESS

Why do smart, capable people wait when they should execute instead? Simply, it's because they choose a losing strategy. They stay stuck because they believe specific and paralyzing lies about readiness. Each lie sounds completely reasonable, and each one keeps you stuck exactly where you are.

Lie #1: "I'll Be Ready When I Know Enough"

This one sounds logical: "I need to learn more before I start."

Reading books, taking courses, researching competitors, analyzing markets: it all feels productive. And it is productive, up to a point. The problem is believing that research is a viable substitute for execution.

Leonardo da Vinci said it plainly: *"I have been impressed with the urgency of doing. Knowing is not enough; we must apply. Being willing is not enough; we must do."*

Knowledge without application is just knowledge, not progress.

You can't learn how to swim by reading about swimming. You can't learn to code by merely reading coding books. You can't learn what the market wants today by reading market research reports from last year's data. You learn by doing. Every time and without exception.

What the Research Shows

In 2000, psychologists Sheena Iyengar of Columbia University and Mark Lepper of Stanford University published a landmark study in the Journal of Personality and Social Psychology. Their finding was counterintuitive: more choices do not lead to better decisions. They lead to paralysis.

Participants who were presented with 24 options were significantly less likely to take action than those given only 6. Even when the larger set contained objectively better options, people froze. The sheer volume of possibilities made deciding feel harder.

This matters because it reveals something fundamental about how we operate. Our brains are not wired to optimize across dozens of variables. We are wired to act on enough information, not all of it.

A 2015 Stanford University study led by researcher Manish Saggar reinforced the point from a different angle. Using brain imaging, the team found that participants who engaged their executive control centers more heavily during a creative drawing task actually produced worse results. The lead researcher summarized it simply: the more you think about it, the more you mess it up (Saggar et al., Scientific Reports, 2015).

Overthinking doesn't sharpen performance. It dulls it. Past a certain threshold, gathering more information does not improve your decisions. It actively degrades them and, in many cases, prevents you from executing at all.

That means: the research loop that feels like preparation is, past a certain point, your brain's method for avoiding the discomfort of executing. It's delay dressed up in a productivity costume.

Jan Koum learned more about developing messaging apps in the first three weeks of WhatsApp's broken launch than he would have learned in three years of research. When his app crashed twelve times in one hour, he didn't simply learn "apps crash sometimes." He learned exactly which memory management pattern caused crashes. And this was knowledge he could only gain by observing real users encountering real problems in real time. When users hacked his status feature to send messages, he didn't just learn "users want messaging." He learned which specific messaging behaviors mattered most, information no research could have revealed.

Reality is the best teacher, but you can only access it by executing first. No amount of preparation puts you in contact with the actual thing.

Lie #2: "I'll Be Ready When Conditions Are Perfect"

The second lie is waiting for ideal circumstances:

"When I have more capital." "When the market is better." "When I have more time." "When the economy stabilizes."

Perfect conditions never arrive. And even if they did, they would create perfect competition. Because if conditions are perfect for you, they are perfect for everyone. When the market is "ready," a thousand competitors flood in simultaneously. Imperfect conditions mean fewer competitors, more urgency, and more opportunity for the person willing to move.

What the Research Shows

A 2010 study led by psychologist Simon Sherry at Dalhousie University examined self-oriented perfectionism among psychology professors at universities across the U.S. and Canada. The results were striking. Professors who demanded perfection of themselves before acting published fewer total papers, fewer first-authored papers, received fewer citations, and placed their work in lower-impact journals. These results held even after the researchers controlled for conscientiousness and other competing variables. The team concluded that self-oriented perfectionism represents a form of counterproductive over-striving, one that limits productivity rather than improving it (Sherry et al., Canadian Journal of Behavioural Science, 2010).

A 2021 scoping review in Frontiers in Psychiatry reinforced this finding, identifying perfectionism as a consistent barrier to professional output across domains (Steinert, Heim, & Leichsenring, 2021).

Jan Koum launched WhatsApp in 2009 during a recession, when unemployment was over 10 percent, and venture capital was scarce. Conventional wisdom said this was a terrible time to build a startup. Still, those imperfect conditions meant less competition, a cost-conscious market where utility mattered more than aesthetics, and hungry users seeking free alternatives to expensive SMS fees.

WhatsApp, Uber, and Airbnb all launched during the economic uncertainty of 2008 to 2010. Not despite bad timing, but in part, because of it. Imperfect conditions filter out those waiting for the right moment, leaving the field open to those willing to execute anyway.

Perfect timing is a story people tell themselves to justify the window of opportunity they're about to miss.

Lie #3: "I'll Be Ready When I Feel Confident"

The third lie is the most seductive, because it sounds the most reasonable. "I'll start when I feel confident." You've been told your entire life that you need to be confident before you can do something significant. So waiting for it feels responsible, not cowardly.

Here is the problem. The sequence is backwards.

Confidence doesn't create action. Action creates confidence. (I'll dig into this later in the book)

Albert Bandura's landmark research on self-efficacy, which I cover in depth in Chapter 5, found that genuine confidence comes from mastery experiences: actually doing the thing, not reading about it or visualizing it. People who acted despite doubt built real confidence through the act itself. People who waited for confidence before acting rarely acted at all.

This isn't a motivational claim. This is a documented psychological mechanism. The person waiting to feel confident before starting is waiting for something that can only be produced by starting. They're waiting for a result that requires the action they are delaying. The wait is infinite by design.

Jan Koum probably didn't feel confident launching an app that wasn't fully functional. He launched anyway. Every small success that followed, fixing the memory leak, watching crash reports drop, seeing users return, then return again, built the confidence that preparation never could have built. The confidence he gained didn't precede the execution. It was produced by it.

You'll rarely ever feel ready to start. Starting always feels uncomfortable. Shifting away from a bad habit to a better one is never comfortable. The first version of something always feels inadequate. The launch always feels too soon. That discomfort isn't a sign you're not ready. It's your signal to execute.

THE OPPORTUNITY COST OF WAITING

Most people who are stuck can justify it in an infinite number of ways, but when they boil it down, the theme is the same. They believe there's no harm in waiting, so they comfortably stay stuck in eternal preparation. So why shouldn't you keep preparing until you eventually feel ready?

Because waiting isn't neutral, it has a cost. And that cost is significant. It's time you can never recover, learning you never accumulate and progress that doesn't get a chance to compound.

Imagine two people with the same goal. Both are equally capable. One waits to feel ready while the other starts now.

The person who waits spends six months researching, six months building a complete product, then launches in month thirteen. They have zero customers, zero feedback, and zero real-world lessons. The person who starts now launches the simplest possible version in month one and spends the next twelve months iterating based on actual feedback. By month thirteen, they have customers, a product shaped by reality rather than assumptions, and a hundred lessons the person who waited hasn't even begun to learn yet.

Now extend that over five years. The gap doesn't close, it widens.

Most people look at that gap and see a difference in results. More customers, more revenue, more momentum. That's true, but it misses the deeper advantage. The person who has been in motion for twelve months has not just accumulated outcomes. They have developed something far harder to replicate: judgment.

They know which systems actually work for their specific situation because they have tested ideas against reality and watched what held up. That kind of knowledge cannot be gathered from a course, a book, or a planning session. It only comes from contact with the real world, repeated over time.

The person still waiting for perfect conditions has none of that. They are not just behind on results. They are behind on the ability to make good decisions, which means every future choice they face will be harder, not easier.

When they read a book about building better habits, they can apply it immediately because they already have a foundation of action to build on. When they encounter a decision-making framework, they have real decisions to reference, not hypothetical ones. The person still preparing is consuming frameworks with nothing to apply them to.

The research on mastery experiences confirms this directly, you'll see the full framework in Chapter 5 but doing the thing is the singular mechanism that builds the self-belief required to keep executing at higher and higher levels. Every day you wait is a day you could be building that belief through execution.

Perfect preparation has infinite cost and finite benefit. Imperfect execution has finite cost and infinite benefit.

THE FIVE PRINCIPLES

Everything in Jan Koum's story maps to the five principles that govern execution. They're not isolated tactics. They're an integrated system, and the rest of this book teaches each principle in depth with specific frameworks you can implement immediately.

Action Creates Clarity: Jan launched a broken app and learned through doing. He didn't wait for clarity. He executed his way toward it.

Identity Drives Results: Jan became an entrepreneur by building, by doing what entrepreneurs do, not by preparing to build.

Discipline Beats Motivation: Jan built and iterated daily regardless of crash logs, bad reviews, or investor dismissal.

Decide Fast, Adjust Faster: Jan made rapid decisions and changed course immediately when user behavior demanded it.

Trust the Invisible Work: Jan persisted through five years of quiet growth that nobody outside his user base was watching.

Here's how the chapters in this book will build on these principles:

Chapter 2: The Execution Mindset. *Why smart people don't execute and how to rewire the conditioning that keeps you waiting.*

Chapter 3: Action Creates Clarity. How to move before you're ready and let clarity emerge through doing.

Chapter 4: Your First Move. How to break the cycle of delay with one committed action.

Chapter 5: Become The Person Now. How to build a new identity through behavior before the outcomes arrive.

Chapter 6: Systems Outlast Feelings. How to build a discipline framework that runs when motivation doesn't.

Chapter 7: Speed Beats Perfection. How to make faster decisions with incomplete information and adjust in real time.

Chapter 8: Trust The Invisible Work. How to persist through the invisible phase when effort precedes evidence.

Chapter 9: Measure What Matters Now. How to measure the inputs that compound before the outputs appear.

Chapter 10: The Complete System. How all five principles function as one integrated system.

Chapter 11: Your First 90 Days. Your specific week-by-week plan to build and run the complete execution system."

YOUR MOMENT OF DECISION

Right now, you're at a fork in the road.

Path 1: Close this book thinking, "That's inspiring, but my situation is different." You convince yourself that Jan Koum had tech skills you don't have, that your circumstances are unique, that you need more preparation, more knowledge, more resources, better timing. Six months from now, you're in the same place you are today. Still planning. Still preparing. Still waiting for conditions that will never be perfect.

Path 2: Close this chapter and take one action toward the goal you've been avoiding. Not a perfect action. Not a complete plan. Just movement. You don't need to know the whole path. You don't need to feel confident. You don't need perfect conditions. You just need to move. Because the clarity you're seeking will emerge from executing. The confidence you're waiting for will follow the actions you take. The only way to become ready is to execute first, before you're ready.

CHAPTER 1 SUMMARY

- **Execution beats preparation**. Jan Koum launched a broken app and built a $19 billion company. Color Labs raised $41 million, and lost $34 million. Same window. Opposite outcomes.
- **The Three Lies of Readiness** keep capable people waiting: you need more knowledge, better conditions, and more confidence. All three are false because knowledge only compounds through taking action. Jan learned more in three weeks of a broken launch than three years of research would have produced. Imperfect conditions reduce competition; WhatsApp, Uber, and Airbnb all launched during the 2008-2010 downturn. Confidence follows action; it never precedes it.
- **The opportunity cost of waiting** isn't just lost results; it's lost judgment. The person in motion for twelve months has

a foundation to apply every framework they encounter, while the person still preparing has nothing to apply them to. That gap compounds and cannot be bought back.

- **Perfect preparation** has infinite cost and finite benefit. Imperfect execution has finite cost and infinite benefit.

WHAT'S NEXT

Chapter 2: The Execution Mindset shows you exactly how to develop the mindset that enables execution. You'll discover why most people resist execution, and exactly how to reprogram yourself for action.

But before you turn the page, ask yourself: What's the one thing you've been preparing for instead of executing? What's stopping you from doing it today?

Write it down. Say it out loud. Acknowledge it.

Because in Chapter 2, we're going to turn that preparation into action.

Let's execute.

2. THE EXECUTION MINDSET

"Act as if what you do makes a difference. It does." —
William James

In the mid-1950s, a former Marine in his late twenties sat in an acting classroom at the Pasadena Playhouse in California, waiting for his grades. The instructor handed back the evaluations, and Gene Hackman had earned the lowest score in the school's history.

This wasn't a borderline assessment. The Pasadena Playhouse was one of America's most respected theater schools. The institution that had trained countless working actors and its instructors had spent entire careers learning to identify talent. Their conclusion about Hackman was unanimous and formally documented: he had no talent whatsoever. Three months after enrolling, the school expelled him. It was the first time the school had ever removed a student for lacking ability. Even his classmates agreed.

Hackman and a fellow student named Dustin Hoffman were jointly designated "Least Likely to Succeed." The instructors explained that Hackman was simply too unconventional. At 27, he was a married

Marine Corps veteran among younger aspiring actors. He didn't look like a leading man, and his presence, in the eyes of every trained professional in the room, was forgettable. What followed his expulsion was over a decade of systematic rejection.

THE WILDERNESS YEARS

Hackman moved to New York and took work as a doorman at an apartment building. One afternoon, a Marine officer from his service years happened to walk through the lobby, looked him over, then said: "Hackman, you're a sorry son of a bitch." At another job he had, waiting tables at Howard Johnson's, a popular restaurant and hotel chain at the time, his former instructor from the Pasadena Playhouse came in for dinner one evening, looked up from the menu, saw Hackman serving food, and remarked: "This job proves you won't amount to anything." Hackman auditioned for Gene Kelly's musical called "Pal Joey," and after Hackman sang, Kelly approached him and offered a polite brush-off that made it clear he hadn't made the cut.

For many years, Hackman worked odd jobs as a shoe salesman, furniture mover, and soda jerk, all while grinding through cattle call auditions he rarely won. The same message arrived on repeat from credentialed professionals who had dedicated their careers to evaluating exactly this: "You're not good enough. You'll never make it. Give up." He had overwhelming evidence supporting these sentiments. He kept showing up anyway.

THE MINDSET DIFFERENCE

Hackman was doing three things that separated him from every classmate who quit after the first few rejections.

First, he had separated his identity from external validation. When his former instructor saw him waiting tables and declared he'd never amount to anything, Hackman didn't update his self-assessment accordingly. He understood, at some fundamental level, that he was an actor because he acted. What someone else decided about that didn't change what he did every day.

Second, he measured success by his inputs rather than outcomes. He couldn't control whether casting directors chose him. He could only control whether he showed up to audition. So that's what he measured. He measured success by attending his audition, even when he knew they would probably turn him away.

Third, he read rejection as valuable information rather than the final destination. Each time a director passed on him, he didn't think, "This proves I have no talent." Instead, he thought, "That director wanted a different type of person." "That character required more intensity." "That audition format didn't show what I bring to the table." The data points accumulated; he adjusted and kept executing.

THE BREAKTHROUGH

In 1967, eleven years after being expelled from the Pasadena Playhouse and now 37 years old, Gene Hackman was cast in Bonnie and Clyde. He won an Academy Award in 1971 for Best Actor in the movie "The French Connection." In 1992, he won an Academy

Award for Best Supporting Actor in the movie "Unforgiven." The man they expelled for having no talent built a career spanning nearly 80 films and became one of the most respected actors of his generation.

And Dustin Hoffman, his "Least Likely to Succeed" classmate who went on to his own legendary career, later explained what those Pasadena instructors had missed. He said Hackman's acting was so natural and unaffected that his teachers didn't recognize it as acting. They expected a theatrical performance, but what Hackman delivered was authentic human behavior. They had never seen it done that way before, so they dismissed him as talentless.

The instructors weren't evaluating him correctly. They were evaluating him against their existing model of what they thought talent looked like. Their model was wrong, and Hackman's execution didn't care.

That's not confidence. That's not willpower. That's an execution mindset.

THE REAL PROBLEM ISN'T YOUR WILLPOWER

You know what you need to do, so why can't you just do it?

That common assumption is that the obstacle is willpower or motivation. That it's discipline in some vague, self-help sense. The belief that if you just wanted it badly enough, you would do something about it. That assumption is wrong. And it's keeping you stuck.

You can't execute consistently because you were systematically trained not to. For the first two decades of your life, every institution you passed through rewired your behavior to wait for permission, avoid failure, seek external validation, and measure yourself by what other people think. This isn't a character flaw; it's conditioning. And fortunately, your conditioning can be reversed and rewired.

WHERE THE CONDITIONING CAME FROM

Three significant institutions helped shape how you relate to execution. Understanding each one is the first step toward undoing it and rebuilding it correctly.

The School System:

From roughly age six to twenty-two, school taught you a specific set of behavioral rules. Wait for permission before acting: raise your hand, wait to be called on, and ask before you do anything. Get it right the first time: you lose points for wrong answers and gain them with correct answers. Failure is penalized rather than celebrated. You always seek expert validation: teachers grade your work and tell you whether or not they think it's good. You avoid mistakes because your GPA will decrease, you may limit your options, and you may signal that you lack ability. This conditioning makes sense in a classroom designed to produce consistent, compliant output, but it's catastrophic in any setting where you're building something new.

In the real world, nobody gives you permission to start. A fitness coach who sits around waiting for someone to call on them before launching their business will never launch. A writer who waits for an authority figure to confirm their work is good enough will never publish a book. An entrepreneur who avoids the mistake of an imperfect first product will never have a product at all. Life doesn't grade on a curve. It only rewards the person who executes, adjusts, and executes again.

Corporate Conditioning:

If you've spent time inside a large organization, you absorbed a second layer of debilitating conditioning. Get approval before acting. Build consensus before deciding. Minimize visible risk. Follow the established process. Document everything in case something fails, and failure is never an option.

Those habits protect organizations that are defending assets they've already built, but they're the opposite of what's required when you're building yourself. The behaviors that kept you employed can be the exact behaviors that prevent you from ever building something of your own. Research by Kathleen Eisenhardt at Stanford found that people who make faster decisions in high-velocity environments consistently outperformed slower, more consensus-driven ones, because they gathered real-time information instead of waiting for certainty.

Social Media:

The most recent layer of conditioning is also the most insidious because it's engineered specifically to exploit your brain's reward circuitry. Social media has taught an entire generation that external validation equates to self-worth. Likes, followers, and comments determine whether your work matters. You start using curated highlights as your benchmark for reality, which makes you believe everyone else succeeds easily while you struggle alone. When you get low engagement, you permit yourself to quit.

This creates a behavioral loop that makes sustained execution nearly impossible. You create something, check the response, and let it determine whether you continue. Your work's actual quality becomes secondary to its performance in the first 24 hours.

Hackman's generation had none of this. He couldn't check how many likes his audition received. He had no daily comparison feed showing which of his Pasadena classmates were further ahead. He just kept executing. That wasn't exceptional willpower. It was the absence of a system designed to make him stop.

Research conducted by Vogel, Rose, and Roberts, published in the journal A study from the Psychology of Popular Media Culture, found that social comparison on digital platforms significantly increases performance anxiety. This anxiety, in turn, decreases the likelihood of individuals engaging in creative or entrepreneurial activities, particularly among those who already feel uncertain about their abilities. The researchers identified this pattern as "validation dependency": a state in which action requires external permission before it feels justified.

WHAT AN EXECUTION MINDSET ACTUALLY IS

An execution mindset isn't confidence, positive thinking, visualization, or affirmation. Those are feeling-states that come and go. An execution mindset is structural. It's a set of operating principles that govern how you interpret the world and what you do next, regardless of how you feel, and it has three main components.

Identity Independence. Your self-concept is determined by what you do, not by what others say about you. Hackman, for example, was an actor because he acted. His instructor's opinion didn't change that. His booking history didn't change that. You are what you do consistently, not what anyone else decides you are.

Process Orientation. You measure success by inputs you control rather than outcomes you don't. Hackman couldn't control whether or not he got cast; he could only control whether he auditioned. Research from the University of Pennsylvania on achievement goals found that people who oriented their effort around the process rather than the outcome showed significantly higher persistence rates when facing obstacles, because they had redefined success as executing the process, not achieving the result.

Evidence Interpretation. You read your setbacks as data points rather than final results. Every rejection contains information: what the market wants, what you need to develop, what approach isn't working. You extract it and adjust. You don't interpret it as proof of your limitations.

WHY KNOWING ISN'T ENOUGH

By now, you understand where your conditioning came from. You can see the school system in how you wait for permission. You can see corporate culture in how you manage by consensus. You can see social media in how you measure your worth by engagement. Understanding all of this is genuinely useful. But it's not enough to change anything by itself.

Here is the problem that most personal development books, including this one, if I'm not explicit enough, run directly into: knowing what to do and actually doing it are governed by two entirely different psychological systems. The first is deliberate and conscious. The second is automatic and situational. You can update the first system by reading, but the second system doesn't respond to reading. It responds to pre-planned triggers.

Think about the last time you intended to do something and didn't. You probably knew exactly what you needed to do. You may have wanted to do it. And when the moment arrived, something else happened instead. You checked your phone. You told yourself you'd start after one more thing. You decided conditions weren't quite right. It wasn't because you lacked information; it was because, in that specific moment, when the resistance showed up, your brain had no pre-loaded instruction for what to do next.

Hackman probably understood this without being able to articulate it. He never waited to feel motivated before walking into a casting office. He never looked for the right moment to audition. Instead, he decided ahead of time how he would handle doubt: he would show up no matter what. He locked that decision in before he ever faced resistance, not in the moment of hesitation. That distinction matters more than anything else. It is the entire mechanism behind his approach.

THE RESEARCH: Peter Gollwitzer at New York University published foundational research in 1999 in American Psychologist, establishing what he called "implementation intentions"-specific if-then plans in the format "When situation X occurs, I will do Y." A 2006 meta-analysis by Gollwitzer and Sheeran examining 94 independent studies with over 8,000 participants found that people who formed implementation intentions were significantly more likely to follow through on intended behaviors than those who formed goal intentions alone, with a medium-to-large effect size (d = 0.65). To put that in plain terms: having a strong goal and having a pre-planned response to the moment when resistance activates are two different things, and the second one roughly doubles your likelihood of actually executing. The mechanism is that the if-then structure bypasses the deliberative system. When the anticipated situation occurs, the brain doesn't have to make any decisions. The decision has already been made. The "if" statement automatically triggers the "then" response. Gollwitzer refers to this concept as "strategic automaticity." Neuroimaging studies confirm that individuals who use implementation intentions exhibit activity in brain regions linked to attention and memory retrieval, as opposed to areas associated with conscious effort. As a result, the behavior becomes more automatic and requires less willpower to start.

This is why every shift in this chapter comes with two components: a practice that tells you what to do, and an if-then plan that tells your brain what to do when resistance specifically shows up. The first is a goal intention. The second is the implementation intention that operationalizes the goal intention.

The five shifts below are pre-loaded behavioral responses to specific triggers. Your conditioning activates in specific moments: when you feel doubt, when you see a metric, when someone criticizes your work, or when you don't feel ready. Each if-then plan targets exactly one of those moments and replaces the conditioned response with a deliberate one.

Read each one, then write your version. The act of writing it in your own words is itself the formation of the implementation intention;

that's when the mental link between the trigger and the response gets encoded in your brain.

You don't overcome conditioning by wanting to. You overcome it by deciding in advance what you will do when it activates, before the moment arrives, when it's still easy to think clearly.

THE FIVE MINDSET SHIFTS

The conditioning you were exposed to has taught you to wait for external permission before you take action. Each of the following shifts reclaims that permission and puts it back in your own hands. They override it, action by action, until the new pattern becomes the default. They don't replace your conditioning overnight, and you won't feel comfortable or natural at first, but that's the point. Over time and with enough reps, you'll rewire your conditioning completely.

Shift 1: From "Feeling Ready" to "Taking Action Anyway"

The old pattern: I'll act when I feel confident.

The new pattern: I act now despite feeling unprepared.

Confidence doesn't create action. Action creates confidence. As I mentioned earlier, Albert Bandura's self-efficacy research established this clearly: the primary source of genuine self-belief is mastery experiences, the accumulation of evidence that you can handle challenges. That evidence only comes from doing the thing. Every time Hackman auditioned, knowing he'd probably be rejected, he was building what I call *Execution Capacity, which is* the proven ability to act in the face of resistance. It's built through repeated acts of doing exactly that. Not because the audition went well. Because he proved to himself that he could act despite fear. That proof, compounded over fourteen years, became a foundation no instructor could erode.

The practice: Identify one action you're avoiding because you don't feel ready, each morning. Commit to taking that action before the end of the day. It doesn't have to be perfect; it just needs to be the action you've been avoiding. Then write your if-then plan for when resistance shows up, because it's certain to.

Your if-then plan: "When I notice I am avoiding something because I don't feel ready, I'll take one step toward it within the next 30 minutes, no matter how small that step is."

Write your specific version: the exact action you keep avoiding. The exact moment when you realize you're avoiding it. The exact smallest step you'll take instead. The more specific your "if" and "then" is, the more automatic your response will be when the moment arrives.

Hackman's version of this would have read: "When I feel the temptation to skip an audition because I'm going to be rejected anyway, I will walk in the door and do the audition." That was not a feeling he cultivated. It was a decision he had already made.

Shift 2: From "Outcome Obsession" to "Process Focus"

The old pattern: success is defined by achieving the outcome I want.

The new pattern: success is defined by executing the process regardless of outcome.

You can't control whether customers buy your product, whether publishers accept your manuscript, or whether investors fund your business. You can control whether you make offers, submit your work, and pitch to investors. When you measure by outcome, most days feel like failure because outcomes lag far behind inputs (I'll dive into this later in the book). When you measure by process, every day you execute is a win.

The practice: Rewrite your current primary goal in process terms. For example, "Get 1,000 followers" becomes "Post daily for 30 days." "Make $10,000 in revenue" becomes "Have 100 sales conversations." "Finish the book" becomes "Write 500 words daily." Only track your process metric. Then write your if-then plan for the moment you feel the pull to check an outcome metric instead.

Your if-then plan: "When I feel the urge to check a result I can't control, follower counts, revenue totals, response rates, I will instead open my process tracker and log whether I executed my daily action today."

The reason outcome-checking is so hard to stop is that it provides a dopamine hit, whether the number went up or down, your brain gets stimulated either way. Your if-then plan redirects it. You still get to check something, and it's something you can control.

Shift 3: From "External Validation" to "Internal Score-keeping"

The old pattern: I'm succeeding if people say I'm succeeding.

The new pattern: I'm succeeding if I'm executing my system.

When the Pasadena Playhouse voted Hackman as the least likely to succeed, that was the external scorecard. If he had accepted it, he would have quit in 1956. Instead, he kept his own score. When he asked himself, "Am I acting?" As long as the answer was yes, he was succeeding, regardless of what any instructor, casting director, or former colleague thought about him.

The practice: Create a four-question scorecard you answer every evening.

1. Did I execute my system today?
2. Did I take action despite resistance?
3. Did I learn something through doing?
4. Did I adjust based on the feedback I received?

Four "yes" answers mean you succeeded. It doesn't matter what any external metric may have shown. Then write your if-then plan for the moment someone's opinion of your work threatens to become your measurement of it.

Your if-then plan: "When I receive criticism or low external feedback on my work, I will open my scorecard before I respond or react, answer the four questions honestly, and let that score determine whether today was a success."

Hackman's scorecard had one question: "Did I act like an actor today?" When his former instructor told him his waiter job proved he'd never amount to anything, Hackman didn't need to argue. He had already kept his own score. The instructor's opinion wasn't a data point he had agreed to measure himself against.

Shift 4: From "Failure as Final" to "Failure as Data"

The old pattern: failure means I should quit.

The new pattern: failure means I learned something I couldn't have learned any other way.

Your school conditioning taught you that failure lowers your GPA and limits your future. In the real world, failure is the mechanism through which you acquire irreplaceable knowledge. A pitch that doesn't land teaches you something about your positioning that no amount of preparation could have revealed. A product nobody buys teaches you about market fit that no research would have shown you. The failure isn't the problem. Failing to extract the lesson is.

The practice: After every failure, complete this sentence before moving on: "This taught me that _______." If you can't complete it, you haven't extracted the data yet. Keep thinking until you can. Every failure contains a lesson. Your job is to find it before you decide how to feel about it. Then write your if-then plan for the moment a failure triggers the impulse to quit.

Your if-then plan: "When something fails and I feel the impulse to stop trying, I will complete the sentence 'This taught me that _______,' before I make any decision about whether to continue."

The sentence is not a trick to make you feel better about failure. It is a forcing function that activates the analytical part of your brain before the emotional part has finished reacting. You can't complete the sentence and simultaneously conclude that your failure is final. The act of extracting the lesson reframes your failure as input before you have decided it's a verdict.

Shift 5: From "Waiting for Permission" to "Claiming Authority"

The old pattern: I need credentials or approval before I can start.

The new pattern: I claim authority through execution, not permission.

Hackman didn't wait for the acting school to certify his talent. He didn't wait for agents to believe in him. He claimed his identity as an actor by acting. His authority came from execution, rather than external validation. This is the direct inversion of your conditioning. You were trained that authority comes from your credentials, such as your grade, your degree, your certification, or your title. In practice, credentials follow competence, and competence only develops through execution.

The practice: Identify one thing you have been waiting to start until you feel qualified enough. Stop asking whether you are allowed to call yourself a writer and start writing daily. Stop asking whether you're qualified to start the business and start serving customers. You're a writer because you write. You're a business owner because you run a business. Then write your if-then plan for the moment your "not qualified yet" voice shows up, because it's likely to show up every time you attempt something that matters.

Your if-then plan: When I catch myself thinking "I'm not qualified enough to do this yet," I will immediately take one action that someone who was already qualified would take," and I'll take it right now, before I talk myself out of it."

The cost of waiting for permission isn't abstract. Every day you don't publish is a day someone else with the same or less knowledge does. Every month you don't start the business is a month someone else is getting the market feedback you need. The authority you're waiting for isn't going to arrive through preparation. It only arrives through the accumulation of evidence that doing the thing gives you. And getting that evidence only starts coming when you start executing.

Hackman didn't wait for the Pasadena Playhouse to certify his talent. He couldn't have. They had formally concluded he had none. He claimed the identity of an actor by acting, and fourteen years later, the Academy of Motion Picture Arts and Sciences confirmed what his own scorecard had said all along.

THE EXECUTION MINDSET DIAGNOSTIC

Use these five questions to identify which conditioning patterns are most active in your life right now. You must be honest. The goal isn't a perfect score. It's to get an accurate diagnosis so you know where you should focus.

> **Question 1:** When you think about starting something new, what comes first? (A) "What if I fail?" or (B) "What's the first action I could take?" If A: focus on Shift 2 and Shift 4.

> **Question 2:** When someone criticizes your work, what do you think? (A) "Maybe they're right, I should quit," or (B) "Interesting. What can I learn from this?" If A: focus on Shift 3 and Shift 4.

> **Question 3:** When you don't feel motivated, what happens? (A) I don't take action, or (B) I execute my minimum system

anyway. (If you don't have a minimum system, I'll break it down later in the book.) If A: focus on Shift 1 and Shift 2.

Question 4: When you look at successful people, what do you think? (A) "They have advantages I don't have" or (B) "They executed consistently over time." If A: focus on Shift 1 and Shift 5.

Question 5: When you're unsure if you're qualified, what do you do? (A) Research more, take courses, wait for credentials, or (B) Execute and let results demonstrate qualification. If A: focus on Shift 5 and Shift 1.

THE 30-DAY REPROGRAMMING PROTOCOL

As I've said, your mindset doesn't change through reading. It changes through repeated action that contradicts your old conditioning. This protocol provides for repetition through a structured daily practice. Each two-week phase will introduce one new practice as the primary focus, but nothing from a previous phase stops; the practices stack. By the end of 30 days, you're going to be doing all three simultaneously, every day, which is precisely the point. Your goal is to build a default operating mode where executing without external validation, measuring by process, and extracting lessons from failure all happen automatically.

Weeks 1 and 2: Identity Independence

Take one action each day that requires zero external validation. For example, write without sharing it, build without showing anyone, practice a skill without an audience. or work on your project without checking any metrics or responses. The goal is to accumulate evidence that you can execute without needing outside confirmation. Document it somewhere you can see it, a journal, a note on your phone, or a dedicated execution log. Continue for all 30 days.

Evening reflection: *"Today I executed without external validation. This proves I can _______."*

Weeks 2 and 3: Process Orientation

Redefine one outcome-based goal as a process-based goal, and only track the process metric. Don't check follower counts, revenue totals, or any outcome metric for two weeks. Track only whether you executed the daily action. The goal is to break the habitual outcome-checking loop and rebuild your measurement system around inputs that you control.

Evening reflection: *"Today, I measured success by my actions. I executed: _______."*

Weeks 3 and 4: Evidence Interpretation

Intentionally take one action designed to generate rejection or failure. Send a cold email that you expect will be ignored. Make an offer you think will be declined. Submit work you think will be rejected. Then extract the lesson immediately. The goal is to build comfort with failure and competence at learning from it: two skills your conditioning systematically suppressed.

Evening reflection: *"Today I failed at: _______. This taught me: _______. My next adjustment: _______."*

All 30 Days: Internal Score-keeping

Answer your four-question scorecard every evening without exception. Did I execute my system? Did I take action despite resistance? Did I learn something through doing? Did I adjust based on feedback? Track your streak. The streak becomes its own form of motivation, but unlike external validation, you control it entirely.

YOUR EXECUTION MINDSET COMMITMENT

Reading this chapter doesn't change anything for you. Writing this down and treating it as a contract with yourself does, and that's not a motivational phrase; it's a well-documented psychological mechanism.

Psychologist Robert Cialdini spent decades studying what makes people follow through on their decisions. In his groundbreaking book *Influence* (1984), he discovered that people feel a powerful internal drive to stay consistent with commitments they have already made. This drive gets even stronger when someone writes the commitment down, makes it voluntarily, and signs their name to it (Cialdini, *Influence: The Psychology of Persuasion*, 1984).When you write something down and you sign it, your brain encodes it as part of your self-image. From that point forward, not following through feels like a violation of who you are. That internal pressure is far more durable than motivation, which fades, or willpower, which depletes. It doesn't require you to feel like doing the thing. It just makes not doing it uncomfortable in a way that staying quiet never would.

This is also why every exercise in this book that ends with a signature line is there by design, not decoration. Each one is a small act of identity commitment, a vote for the person you are choosing to become. The research is consistent: the act of writing and signing is itself the beginning of the behavioral change. Not the end of a chapter. The beginning of what comes next.

I commit to developing an execution mindset by:

- **Acting before I feel ready.** The specific action I will take within 24 hours despite feeling unprepared:

  ____

- **Measuring process, not outcomes.** My current outcome-based goal, rewritten as a process metric:

  ____

- **Keeping my own score.** My four daily yes/no questions:

  ____

- **Interpreting failure as data.** The next time I fail, I will complete this sentence before moving on: "This taught me that ______."

- **Claiming authority through action.** I will stop waiting for permission to ______ and claim that identity by doing ______ today.

Signature: ______________________________________

Date: ______________________

CHAPTER 2 SUMMARY

- You were conditioned to wait for permission, avoid failure, and measure yourself by what others think. Three institutions shaped that conditioning: the school system taught you to wait to be called on, corporate culture taught you to build consensus before deciding, and social media taught you that external validation determines whether your work matters.

- An execution mindset overrides conditioning through three operating principles: Identity Independence-"you are what you do, not what others say"; Process Orientation-"success is executing the process, not achieving the outcome"; and Evidence Interpretation-"setbacks are data, not verdicts."

- Knowing what to do and actually doing it are governed by different systems. The deliberate system responds to reading and the automatic system responds only to pre-planned triggers. Gollwitzer's implementation intention research, comprising 94 studies and 8,000 participants, found that if-then plans roughly double follow-through compared to goal intentions alone. Every mindset shift in this chapter includes one.

- The five shifts are pre-loaded responses to specific resistance moments: act before you feel ready, measure process, not outcomes; keep your own score; read failure as data; and claim authority through execution rather than waiting for permission.

- The 30-Day Protocol stacks these practices across three phases: identity independence in weeks one and two, process orientation in weeks two and three, and evidence interpretation in weeks three and four. The practices do not stop at the end of each phase; they stack. By Day 30, all three are running simultaneously.

- Cialdini's research on commitment and consistency confirms that written, voluntary, signed commitments create internal pressure to follow through that outlasts motivation. The commitment block at the end of this chapter is not a ritual. It is the mechanism.

WHAT'S NEXT

Chapter 3 will show you exactly how to apply your execution mind-set to generate clarity through action, even when you have no idea what you're doing or where you're going.

Complete the commitment above before you turn the page. Not as a ritual. Because the act of writing and signing it is itself an exercise in claiming authority through execution.

Let's execute.

PRINCIPLE 1:
ACTION CREATES CLARITY

3. ACTION CREATES CLARITY

"How do I know what I think until I see what I say?" —
E.M. Forster, *Aspects of the Novel*

On the morning of May 5, 2003, Reid Hoffman clicked "publish" on LinkedIn's homepage and immediately felt sick.

The platform looked unfinished, and profile pages resembled mid-1990s web design: basic text fields, crude layout, and no visual refinement. There was no messaging system, no groups feature, no company pages, and no job board. Just three core functions: create a profile, connect with people, and manage your contacts. That was it.

For months, his co-founders had pushed him to wait. "Just six more weeks," they said at every planning meeting. "Let's add messaging. Let's polish the design. Let's build the job search feature. Let's make this actually look professional before we launch." His investors were skeptical. "This looks too basic, Reid. You're going to get destroyed in reviews. Wait until it's actually ready." Reid decided to launch anyway.

THE FIRST MONTH

The first month brought 4,500 sign-ups. In Silicon Valley in 2003, when Friendster, another social network, was adding hundreds of thousands of users monthly. LinkedIn's numbers were underwhelming to say the least. The feedback arriving in user emails confirmed the critics' concerns. Users asked where the messaging feature was, why they couldn't see who viewed their profile, and whether this was really all the platform did.

Most founders would have panicked. Most would have concluded they'd launched too early and retreated to build more features before trying again. But Reid did something different. He watched.

He pulled up the user behavior data and studied it obsessively. Not what users were saying they wanted in complaint emails. What they were actually trying to do on the platform. Every click. Every attempted action. Every point where users tried to access something that the platform didn't yet support.

Within two weeks, patterns emerged that no amount of planning could have produced. Users clicked on empty profile sections, trying to add information LinkedIn hadn't even built fields for yet. They messaged connections through workarounds: embedding notes in connection requests and copying external email addresses. They searched for skills and job titles LinkedIn hadn't indexed. They clicked on company names expecting pages that didn't exist. They tried to endorse connections for specific capabilities, and nobody on the team had ever even discussed that idea.

That's when Reid saw the whole project differently. The incomplete platform wasn't a failure. It was telling him exactly what to build next, not what he assumed users needed, and not what they'd claimed they wanted in some survey. He could see what they were actually trying to do, right now, on a live product. That kind of insight doesn't come from a whiteboard. It only shows up when real people use a real thing.

THE PRODUCT MEETING

During week three, Reid called his team together. They gathered, expecting a difficult conversation, possibly a pivot, possibly an admission that the launch had failed. Instead, Reid put the user's behavioral data on the screen.

"I asked you all here to discuss what we should build next," he told them. "But I'm not going to give you my opinion. The users are going to tell us." He walked them through every pattern in the data. "Look at what they're trying to do that we're not letting them do. They're clicking here expecting to message connections directly. They're searching here for skills we haven't indexed. We don't need to guess what to build next. We just need to watch what they're already trying to do."

The team built messaging in weeks. They added company pages, skill indexing, and the features users were already attempting to access. None of it was in Reid's original plan. He couldn't have predicted it. He couldn't have designed those features by thinking harder or planning longer.

The clarity came from launching before it was ready, then watching what happened. The path revealed itself as Reid walked down it.

THE OUTCOME

Within two years of that imperfect launch, LinkedIn had 4 million users. Within five years: 37 million users. In 2011, LinkedIn went public. And in June 2016, Microsoft acquired LinkedIn for $26.2 billion. At the time of writing, LinkedIn has over 1 billion registered members across more than 200 countries.

The feature set that built that company didn't exist in Reid's mind on May 5, 2003. It emerged through thousands of iterations driven by actual user behavior. LinkedIn hadn't designed a billion-dollar product; they discovered it, one incomplete launch at a time.

If Reid had waited until LinkedIn was complete before launching, he never would have launched. Complete is a moving target. The market changes, user needs evolve, technology shifts, and by the time you build your complete vision, reality has moved on, and you've built the wrong thing.

Reid learned what LinkedIn needed to become by launching what it wasn't yet.

Clarity isn't a prerequisite for action; it's a product of it.

THE CLARITY INVERSION

What Reid Hoffman demonstrated has a name, and I call it the Clarity Inversion: the clarity you are waiting for only exists on the other side of the action you're avoiding taking.

I call it the Clarity Inversion because it reverses the sequence most people assume: that you need to understand fully first, then you can act. And research on how humans actually generate understanding in novel situations confirms it works this way.

This isn't a motivational idea. It is a functional description of how you generate clarity. The conventional assumption is that clarity enables action: you understand the situation fully, decide what to do, and execute. That sequence feels logical because it's how you were taught to approach problems when you were younger.

The Clarity Inversion reverses that sequence entirely. In novel situations, the ones where you actually need clarity most, the only way to generate it is through action. You execute first, and understanding follows the movement.

The person who endlessly plans, waits for certainty before moving, which never arrives, so neither does action. The executor moves without certainty, and the movement produces the understanding that the *planner* was waiting to think their way to.

Reid's brain couldn't predict that users would try to send messages through connection requests, that company pages would become critical, or that skill endorsements would drive engagement. Three weeks of real users on an incomplete platform made it all obvious. His clarity came into existence through the act of launching.

WHY THE CLARITY INVERSION WORKS: THREE MECHANISMS

Understanding why the Clarity Inversion works turns "I don't know what to do" from a reason to wait into a signal that you need to move. There are three specific mechanisms through which action generates clarity.

Mechanism 1: Behavioral Revelation

People do not know what they want until they interact with something real. This isn't a cynical observation about human nature. It's a documented fact about how preferences form.

When Reid surveyed potential users in 2002 about what features a professional networking platform needed, they gave him generic answers: find colleagues, see work history, and maybe email them. Those answers didn't tell him anything useful. But when he launched the basic platform, users revealed their actual needs through their behavior. They tried to send messages. They wanted to endorse specific skills. They didn't just browse. They searched for precise capabilities.

What people say they want versus what they do when they're given something real to interact with is usually different. The gap between them is where the most valuable clarity lives, but it only becomes visible through taking action. Instead of surveying 50 people about what features your product should have. Build one core feature and observe which other features they try to access. Don't interview customers about what service they'd buy. Make one specific offer and see if they actually pay. If you're trying to figure out whether a morning workout routine will work for you, get up and do something physical for 10 minutes tomorrow rather than just researching a workout. What you actually do, and don't do, will tell you more about your constraints, energy levels, and preferences than a month of planning ever could. True behavioral revelation only happens through action, never through conversation or internal deliberation.

Mechanism 2: Failure Specificity

Failure from action teaches you exactly what's wrong. Failure to act teaches you nothing.

Reid's incomplete platform "failed" in specific, actionable ways. Users tried to message but couldn't, so he built a messaging system. Users searched for skills but found nothing indexed, so he added skill indexing. Users expected company information but saw blank pages, so he built company pages. Each failure pointed precisely to what to build next.

Compare this to the person who never launches because they're afraid of failure. They experience zero specific failures, so they learn nothing specific. Vague fear is useless. "I'm afraid it won't work" doesn't give you a next step. There's nowhere to go with that. But a specific failure? That's a different thing entirely. "I launched, and twelve people tried to message each other, but the feature doesn't exist." Now you know exactly what to build next.

Generic fear keeps you frozen, but specific failure hands you a map.

Mechanism 3: Iteration Acceleration

Each action creates a new baseline for the next action. Thinking creates no baseline. It just generates more thinking.

From LinkedIn's May 2003 launch, Reid's iteration timeline looked like this: users revealed a messaging need in May and June, the messaging feature was added in July, messaging usage revealed a need for better search in August, search was improved in September, and search patterns revealed a need for skill endorsements in October.

Each action generated data for the next. The product evolved through hundreds of cycles of launch, observe, and adjust.

Now consider what happens if Reid spends those same six months thinking and planning instead of launching. May, June, July, August, September, October: still thinking, no new real data, no new baseline, and no iteration. Zero learning cycles completed.

Stefan Thomke at Harvard Business School found that companies that processed iterations rapidly achieved significantly faster learning velocity than those that optimized for perfection in each cycle. Short-loop experimentation: launching something imperfect, observing what happens, and adjusting quickly to correct course before market conditions shift. Long-cycle perfection: spending months refining before releasing anything, locks in assumptions that may no longer be valid by the time you launch. One imperfect iteration every three days gives you 120 learning cycles per year. One polished iteration every two weeks gives you 26. Learning compounds and compounding requires velocity.

THE ACTION-CLARITY FRAMEWORK

Understanding the Clarity Inversion is necessary, but having a system to apply it consistently is what actually moves you forward. Here is my five-step framework for generating clarity through action.

Step 1: The 5-Minute Data Dive

Before taking any action, spend exactly five minutes identifying the one specific thing you need reality to answer. Not what you need to know to feel confident, but the one question that action can answer and planning can't.

Reid's five-minute question was likely: "Will people actually create professional profiles and connect with colleagues if I give them the absolute minimum viable tool?" That's it. One question. Specific and testable, meaning you'll know within a defined time frame whether the answer is yes or no. He'd know the answer within weeks of launching.

Write down your one question right now:

"The one thing I need to learn through action is: _____________"

Keep it specific and testable. You'll know within a defined time frame whether the answer is yes or no. "I need to learn if my business will work" is too vague. "I need to learn if 10 people will pay $50 for this specific service" is specific and testable. "I need to learn if I can be an entrepreneur" is unanswerable by any single action. "I need to learn if I can make 20 outreach calls this week without quitting" is immediate and self-contained.

Step 2: The Minimum Viable Action

Design the smallest possible action that will answer your five-minute question. Not the smallest action that feels comfortable. The smallest action that generates real data from the external world.

Reid's MVA was launching LinkedIn with profiles and connections only: no messaging, no groups, and no visual polish. Just enough to see if people would create profiles and connect.

Your MVA must meet four criteria:

1. It must involve the external world (not just internal planning)
2. It must generate measurable, observable feedback you can learn from.
3. It must be executable within 72 hours (if it takes longer, it isn't minimal.)
4. And it must feel slightly uncomfortable. If it feels entirely safe, it probably isn't testing anything real.

For example, if you're starting a coaching business, message 10 people today and offer one free 30-minute session. Don't build a website first. Don't design a logo. Message ten people.

If you're writing a book, write 500 words of actual manuscript today and share it with one person for honest feedback. Not an outline. Actual writing.

If you're launching a product, create a one-page description and send it to twenty people, asking if they would pay a specific price for it.

Step 3: Execute Within 72 Hours

This is non-negotiable. If you don't execute your MVA within 72 hours, you're not using this framework. You're just reading about it.

The 72-hour rule isn't arbitrary. Research on the intention-to-action gap shows that momentum decays rapidly. The clarity from your five-minute data dive is perishable. If you wait too long, and it evaporates, it's replaced by doubt and the expanding complexity your brain layers onto a simple action the longer you delay. Philip Sheeran's research on intention and behavior found consistent gaps between forming an intention and following through. The gaps widen the longer the delay. Paul Steel's meta-analysis of more than 200 procrastination studies found that waiting for better conditions is a self-reinforcing loop. Each successful delay increases the likelihood of future delays. The perfect moment you're waiting for diminishes at exactly the rate you approach it.

Set your execution deadline right now: "I will execute [your MVA] by [specific date and time within 72 hours]." Put it in your calendar. Tell someone about it. Make it real and external.

Step 4: Extract the Lesson

After executing your MVA, spend ten minutes extracting the specific lesson. Not "it worked" or "it didn't work." The specific things you learned that inform the next action.

Reid's week-one lessons may have looked like this: people will create profiles even without messaging, which validated the core hypothesis. Users are clearly trying to message each other, which identifies the next build priority. 4,500 sign-ups show market appetite but not viral growth yet, which calibrated his expectations. This professional audience behaves differently from other social networks, which sharpened positioning. Each lesson pointed to a specific next action.

Your four extraction questions:

- What specific behavior did I observe?
- What does this tell me about what to build, do, or change next?
- What assumption did this validate or invalidate?
- What is my next MVA based on this data?

Step 5: Iterate Immediately

Take your extracted lesson and design the next MVA. Don't wait. Don't deliberate. Don't seek permission. Execute now.

Iteration velocity beats iteration quality. Reid added LinkedIn's messaging feature within weeks of launch, not months. It wasn't perfect, but it generated immediate feedback on how users wanted to communicate, which informed the next iteration. This's how the Clarity Inversion compounds: each action generates clarity for the next, which in turn generates clarity for the one after that, building a learning engine that accelerates over time.

THREE MYTHS THE CLARITY INVERSION DESTROYS

There are three prevalent myths about the conventional assumption you need to understand before you can execute. Applying the Clarity Inversion renders them powerless.

Myth 1: "I need more information before I start"

The specific information you actually need is only available on the other side of the action you're avoiding. It doesn't exist in any book, course, or research report. It only comes into existence after you've executed. Reid didn't need to know what all of LinkedIn's features should be before launching. He needed to launch first to discover what features users would actually need. You can read a hundred books about building a business, but none of them will tell you if your specific customers will pay your specific price for your specific offer. That answer only exists in the actual market, and the market only answers when you show up in it.

Myth 2: "I need a plan before I start"

A plan feels like a prerequisite because it creates the sensation of control. If you can see all the steps in sequence, it feels safe to take the first one. But in any genuinely new situation, such as a new business, a new skill, or a new creative project, the steps after the first one don't exist yet. They depend on what happens when you take the first one.

When Reid launched LinkedIn, he had a three-feature platform, not a product roadmap. The roadmap emerged from users' actions. Messaging wasn't in the plan; it was users messaging each other that created it by using workarounds. Users clicked on company names expecting pages that didn't exist because company pages didn't exist yet. Skill endorsements weren't there, users tried to endorse each other, and the team watched. Every step after the launch came from the previous one.

The plan you're waiting to write isn't clarifying your direction. It's just deferring the only thing that actually would: contact with reality. You do not need the full sequence before you take the first step. You need the first step. Then the second step becomes visible from there.

Myth 3: "Successful People Started With All The Answers"

LinkedIn's billion-dollar feature set emerged from thousands of iterations driven by real user behavior over two decades. Nobody starts with clarity. What looks like vision from the outside is almost always iteration from the inside. People who execute first generate clarity through movement and action. People who endlessly plan wait for clarity that never arrives because the only place it exists is on the other side of the action they're still preparing to take.

YOUR 72-HOUR CLARITY INVERSION CHALLENGE

Now you understand the Clarity Inversion, and you have the five-step framework. None of it matters until you apply it.

Hour 1, right now: Complete your five-minute data dive. "The one thing I need to learn through action is: ________________ "

Hours 2 to 24: Design your MVA. "The smallest action that will answer my question is: ________________ " Set your deadline: "I will execute this by [date] at [time]."

Hours 24 to 72: Execute your MVA.

Hour 72: Extract your lesson. "What I learned: ________________ " Then immediately: "My next MVA based on this learning: ________________ "

The reason the challenge ends with your next MVA is intentional. The Clarity Inversion is not a single action. It is a continuous loop. One action generates clarity for the next. You don't stop at one iteration. You build the habit of perpetual movement.

CHAPTER 3 SUMMARY

- **The Clarity Inversion is the core mechanism:** the clarity you are waiting for only exists on the other side of the action you are avoiding. Reid Hoffman didn't build LinkedIn by knowing what it should become. He launched incomplete and let reality tell him.

- **Action generates clarity through three mechanisms**: behavioral revelation shows you what people actually do rather than what they say they want; failure specificity gives you a precise map of what to build next; and iteration acceleration means 120 imperfect cycles per year compounds faster than 26 perfect ones.
- **The five-step framework converts the principle into practice**. Identify the one question only action can answer. Design the smallest action that generates real data. Execute within 72 hours. Extract the specific lesson. Iterate immediately.

WHAT'S NEXT

Chapter 4 gives you a specific challenge to close the gap between understanding and doing. You've learned the Clarity Inversion. Now it's time to use it, with a concrete commitment and a 72-hour deadline.

Let's execute.

4. YOUR FIRST MOVE

"Well done is better than well said." — *Benjamin Franklin*

In 1999, David Goggins finished another night shift as an exterminator and pulled into the Steak' n Shake parking lot. It was the same routine every morning after spraying for cockroaches from 11 PM to 7 AM: a large chocolate milkshake, then across the street to 7-Eleven for a box of mini donuts. During his 45-minute drive home, he ate the entire box, popping them, as he later described, "like Tic Tacs."

He was 24 years old, 297 pounds, making $1,000 a month, and every morning the routine ended the same way: he parked in front of the apartment and felt the weight of knowing he had become exactly what everyone said he would be. Nothing.

His childhood had been brutal. He endured severe beatings from his father. He was diagnosed with a learning disability in third grade, and he developed a stutter from the stress and trauma. He was one of only a handful of Black families in his small Indiana town, where there was a local Ku Klux Klan presence. He tried to escape through the military, but had to leave Air Force pararescue training after being diagnosed with sickle cell trait.

Now he was spraying for pests, eating himself into an early grave, and watching his life disappear one donut at a time.

THE DECISION

One morning, Goggins came home from his shift and turned on the TV, cranking the volume so he could hear it over the shower.

Through the sound of water hitting his ears, he caught fragments of what was playing: "Navy SEALs... toughest training... freezing water... Hell Week..."

He turned off the water and walked into the living room, dripping wet. On the screen was footage of Hell Week: men in the Pacific Ocean, hypothermic, carrying boats on their heads, crawling through mud, some collapsing from exhaustion. Five and a half days of the most brutal military training on earth, designed to break anyone not truly committed.

Goggins stood there, 297 pounds, staring at men who represented everything he wasn't, and he made a decision. Not a plan. Not a goal. Not a "someday I'll get in shape and try that." He decided, *I'm going to become a Navy SEAL.*" Right then, at 297 pounds, unable to run a quarter mile, unable to do a single pull-up, with no swimming ability and no qualifications. He didn't wait to feel prepared or ready. He picked up the phone the next morning and started calling Navy recruiters.

The first one laughed at him. "Can you even swim?" The second one just hung up on him. As Goggins later recalled: "When you tell a recruiter that you're almost 300 pounds and you want to be a SEAL, it doesn't go too well. I got hung up on a lot."

Most people would have stopped there. The rejection would have confirmed what they already believed: I'm not ready. I need to lose weight first. I'll call back when I'm in better shape.

Goggins kept calling. After two weeks, one recruiter agreed to meet with him, and he made a deal that was brutal but simple: lose 106 pounds in three months and pass the ASVAB, the Armed Services Vocational Aptitude Battery, with a higher score than he'd gotten before he joined the Air Force. If he could do that, he'd get his shot at SEAL training.

MOVING BEFORE READY

Goggins had zero experience with weight loss, zero knowledge of nutrition science, and no training plan. He just started moving. The very next day, still 297 pounds, still completely unprepared, he went for a run. He made it a quarter mile before his body gave out. Most people would have thought, "This is impossible." I can't even run a quarter mile. How am I supposed to become a Navy SEAL? Goggins thought differently: "Yesterday I couldn't run at all. Today I ran a quarter mile. Tomorrow I'll run slightly farther." He didn't wait for clarity or understanding of how to become a SEAL. He executed, and the clarity came from executing.

His approach was extreme: consume roughly 800 to 1,000 calories while burning over 5,000 through all-day training. As he explained: "I knew that if I stopped training or became stagnant, I wouldn't be burning any calories, so I just basically trained all day long." Was it the optimal approach? Probably not. Was it sustainable long-term? Definitely not. Did it work? Absolutely.

A major component of being a SEAL is swimming, but he couldn't swim. So he got in the pool and worked through lap after humiliating lap until it started feeling less impossible. He couldn't do a pull-up. So he hung from the bar until his hands bled, then hung some more. Every day, he learned what worked by doing it badly, then doing it slightly less badly the next day.

In less than three months, Goggins lost 106 pounds. From 297 to 191. Not because he had a perfect plan. Because he executed before he was ready and adjusted based on real-life feedback.

THE HELL WEEKS

In 2001, Goggins arrived at Basic Underwater Demolition/SEAL training (BUD/S), but his rapid weight loss had damaged his body. "When you go from 297 pounds to 191 pounds in that time period, and you're running, you're starting to break yourself," he explained. "So I broke myself before I even got into Navy SEAL training."

During his first Hell Week, stress fractures and pneumonia forced him to drop out. The Navy rolled him back, restarting BUD/S training from scratch, and gave him another shot. He made it back to Hell Week a second time before a fractured kneecap ended that attempt too. A third rollback. A third restart. In less than a year, Goggins attempted Hell Week again.

Most people would have read those situations as failures, as proof they weren't meant to be a SEAL, that they had moved too fast, or that they needed more preparation. Goggins read his two failures as data points showing what he needed to fix. He graduated from BUD/S training with Class 235 on August 10, 2001. He later became the only member of the U.S. Armed Forces to complete SEAL training, Army Ranger School, and Air Force Tactical Air Controller training. He went on to complete more than 60 ultra-distance races and, in 2013, set a Guinness World Record with 4,030 pull-ups in 17 hours.

None of that happened because Goggins waited until he felt ready. He moved before he was prepared, paid attention to what each failure was telling him, and adjusted.

The system operates from the most extreme possible starting point: zero preparation, zero competence, and zero favorable conditions. Goggins' story isn't an inspiration story; it's a stress test. If the system worked for David Goggins at 297 pounds in just three months with no training plan, it will work for you.

WHY MOST PEOPLE STILL WON'T EXECUTE

You have three chapters' worth of evidence, you understand the Clarity Inversion, and now you've read how Goggins completely changed the trajectory of his life. Yet there's still a high probability you haven't moved, and it's likely that the reason you haven't is what I'll explain to you next.

Five specific obstacles arise between the moment you understand something and the moment you act on it. You've seen where they come from in earlier chapters. What you need to know now is how to override each one when it activates.

Here is what each obstacle looks like in the moment, along with the one move that neutralizes it.

When you catch yourself researching instead of doing:

You identify something you want to do. Immediately, your brain generates a list of things you "need" to do first: research more, take a course, read these books, build this website, create this plan, wait for better timing. Each item feels productive and necessary.

The research has already given you what it can. The remaining information only exists outside, in the world.

Here's the test that reveals whether something is preparation or procrastination: Does it involve the external world? Other humans, real feedback, actual results? Reading about starting a business is preparation. Calling potential customers is execution. Taking a course on content creation is preparation. Publishing one piece of content and observing what happens is execution.

The fix: When you catch yourself preparing, ask, "What's the smallest external action I could take right now?" Then do that instead.

When you catch yourself waiting to be competent

You believe you need to be good at something before you try it. "I'm not ready to start that project, I don't know enough yet." "I can't publish content, I'm not an expert." This sounds responsible, but it's actually paralyzing.

Competence doesn't come from studying until you're competent. It comes from doing something incompetently, extracting lessons, and doing it slightly less incompetently the next time. K. Anders Ericsson, the cognitive psychologist whose work on expert performance basically launched the whole "10,000 hours" conversation, spent decades studying how people get great at what they do. His conclusion across every field he looked at — music, chess, medicine

— was the same. Deliberate practice in real conditions beats theoretical preparation every time. Goggins wasn't a runner when he started. He became one by running badly for months until he wasn't bad anymore.

The fix: Reframe the goal from "be competent" to "become competent through action." Execute badly. Learn. Execute slightly less badly. Repeat.

When you catch yourself waiting for better conditions

"When I have more money." "When I have more time." "When conditions are better." I've said all of these. You probably have too. And the perfect conditions we're waiting for? They never show up.

A large-scale review of procrastination research found something most of us probably already feel but don't want to admit — waiting for the right moment trains your brain to keep waiting. It works like this: you put something off, and nothing bad happens immediately. So your brain files that away. The delay worked. Next time a decision comes up, the hesitation kicks in a little faster and feels a little more justified. Before long, you've built a habit out of standing still and convinced yourself it's a great strategy.

The worst part is that the ideal moment you're holding out for keeps changing shape. You get close to what you thought the right conditions looked like, and suddenly, there's a new requirement. A new reason it's not quite time yet. The finish line was painted on a truck. It was never going to stay where you first saw it.

Goggins didn't have perfect conditions. He weighed 297 pounds, had three months instead of years, worked as a pest exterminator, and had never completed a significant athletic achievement. But he had one thing: the willingness to start with what he had from where he was.

The fix: Name the condition you're waiting for. Now ask: *"If that condition never arrived, would I never start?"* If the answer is yes, the condition isn't a requirement; it's an excuse that's been elevated to a requirement. Strip it back to the bare minimum you need, then launch the moment you reach it.

When you catch yourself waiting to feel confident

"I'll start when I feel confident." The problem is that confidence doesn't create action. Action creates confidence. Albert Bandura's foundational research on self-efficacy established that mastery experiences, the accumulation of evidence that you can handle challenges, are the primary source of self-belief. That evidence only comes from performing the thing, not from preparing to perform it.

This isn't a new observation. K. Anders Ericsson, whose deliberate practice research is mentioned above, found the same mechanism operating in every domain he studied: repeated performance attempts in real conditions built both competence and the self-belief required to keep going. The two compounds together. You get slightly better, which makes you slightly more willing to try again, which makes you slightly better again. At 0.3 miles, Goggins probably didn't feel confident. He probably felt like he was dying. After 10 runs, he felt slightly less uncertain. After 30, he felt a little more capable. After 100, he felt confident. That progression wasn't a coincidence or a character trait. It was the documented output of accumulated action, exactly what Ericsson's research predicts and exactly what Bandura's earlier work established as the primary mechanism of self-efficacy. The principle is consistent across the research. You're not waiting to feel confident; you're waiting for something that only action produces.

The fix: Every time you think "I'll do it when I feel confident," replace it with "I'll feel confident after I do it ten times." Then do it once.

When you catch yourself doing more research

You keep researching, reading, and learning, but never executing. "Just let me read one more book." "Let me watch a few more videos." Learning feels productive because it creates the sensation of progress without feeling the risk of failure.

But research has sharply diminishing returns. The information you gain from reading provides foundational context, while the knowledge that actually improves your performance comes only from real-world execution and feedback. One bad attempt teaches you more than hours of additional preparation. Brown, Roediger, and McDaniel spent years studying how people retain and apply knowledge, and their findings were clear. Actively doing something and applying what you've learned in real situations beats passive studying every time. Re-reading your notes, watching another tutorial, reviewing the plan one more time, none of it comes close to the learning you get from just trying and falling short.

The fix: Decide in advance how much research is enough. Set the limit before you start. *I'll research for two hours and then execute regardless of remaining uncertainty.* The limit you can't cross: any research that could be replaced by simply doing the thing. If the answer is available by acting, stop researching and act.

The 72-Hour Challenge below converts all five of these overrides into a single mechanical sequence. Once you run it, the obstacles lose most of their power, because you'll have already moved before they have time to compound.

THE 72-HOUR CHALLENGE

Now you have both the proof and the pattern recognition. Here is the complete mechanical system that converts understanding into action, every time, in any domain. You should be able to complete it in 72 hours or less.

Hour 1: The Clarity Question

Set a timer for five minutes and answer this one question: "What's the one thing I need to learn that only action can teach me?"

Not "What do I need to know?" but "What do I need to learn through doing?" This is the difference Goggins understood instinctively: he didn't ask "How do I become a SEAL?" He asked, "Can I run at 297 pounds?" One question was unanswerable by planning. The other could only be answered by putting on his shoes.

"I need to know if my business idea is good" is unanswerable without action. "I need to learn if 10 people will pay $50 for this specific service" is answerable within 72 hours. It requires you to go ask people to buy your shoes for $50. "I need to know if I can be successful" produces nothing. "I need to learn if I can make 20 outreach calls this week without quitting" is answerable only by actually doing it.

Write your Clarity Question right now: "I need to learn: _________ "

Hours 2 to 12: The Minimum Viable Action

Design the smallest possible action that answers your Clarity Question. Not the smallest action that feels comfortable. The smallest action that generates real data from the external world.

Goggins's MVA was direct: run tomorrow morning, even if only a quarter mile, even if you have to walk most of it. Generate real feedback about whether this is physically possible at 297 pounds. It was minimal, viable, and answered his question.

Like in Chapter 3, your MVA must meet four criteria. It must involve the external world, not just internal planning. It must generate measurable, observable feedback you can learn from. It must be executable within 72 hours; if it takes longer, it isn't minimal. And it must feel slightly uncomfortable. If it feels entirely safe, it probably isn't testing anything significant or meaningful.

Examples: if you're starting a coaching business, message 10 people today, offering 1 free 30-minute session. Not a website or a logo. Just ten messages. If you're writing a book, write 500 words of actual writing today and send it to one person for honest feedback. If you're launching a product, write a one-page description and send it to twenty people, asking if they'd pay a specific price for it.

Create your MVA right now: "The smallest action that will answer my question is: ___________________ *"*

"I will complete this by [specific date and time within 72 hours]: ___________________ *"*

Hours 12 to 72: The Execution Zone

This is where most people fail. They complete hours one through twelve. They have a clarity question and a plan, then they don't execute.

Three patterns destroy execution during this window. First, the MVA expands: "one workout" becomes "the perfect workout with ideal equipment and flawless form." Second, fear intensifies as the deadline approaches. Third, the excuses multiply and compound: "I'm too busy today" becomes "I'll do it next week" becomes "maybe this wasn't a good idea." These three interventions will guarantee execution.

Intervention #1: Tell someone what you're doing and when you'll be doing it. Text or call one person right now and tell them: "I'm doing [your MVA] by [specific time]. I'll text you when it's done." Research on commitment devices and accountability consistently finds that public commitment significantly increases follow-through. When you've told someone, not doing so has a social cost. That cost motivates action when internal motivation wavers.

Intervention #2: Prepare the environment before the execution window. Remove all obstacles before the moment arrives: have your equipment ready, gather contact information, prepare your workspace, and eliminate every decision point that could introduce friction. Every "let me just quickly..." that precedes your MVA is a potential abort point. Eliminate them in advance.

Intervention #3: Use the two-minute rule. When it's time to execute, commit only to two minutes. "I'll work on this for two minutes. If I want to stop after two minutes, I can." You won't stop. Starting is the hard part. Once you're in motion, continuing is easy.

The two-minute commitment removes the psychological weight of "all of it" and replaces it with "just this much."

Hours 72 to 73: The Extraction Protocol

Immediately after executing, spend ten minutes extracting the specific lesson. Not "how did it feel" but "what did I learn that I could not have learned any other way?"

Goggins's extraction after his first quarter-mile run might have looked like this:

Behavior observed: ran 0.3 miles before the body stopped. Shoes caused blisters. Morning timing felt better than expected.

What this tells me: I can start running at this weight. I need better shoes. Morning is the time.

Assumption validated: I can begin right now.

Assumption invalidated: I thought I needed to lose some weight before running was even possible.

Next MVA: run in better shoes tomorrow morning again, try for 0.4 miles.

Notice that each answer points to a specific next action. That's the extraction protocol working correctly.

Your four extraction questions after every MVA:

- What specific behavior did I observe? (What actually happened, not what you expected)

- What does this tell me about what to do next? (One specific next action)
- What assumption did this validate or invalidate? (What you thought was true vs. what actually is)
- What is my next MVA based on this data? (Define it before you stop)

Write your extraction answers after executing. Within 24 hours, or you'll lose the specific details that make the data useful.

THE INFINITE LOOP

The 72-Hour Challenge isn't something you do once to prove you can. It's how you operate permanently.

The loop: Clarity Question, MVA design, execute within 72 hours, extract lessons, define next MVA, repeat. Each cycle generates data that informs the next cycle. That's how Goggins went from 297 pounds to completing over 60 ultra-distance races. That's how Koum built WhatsApp from a broken app to a $19 billion acquisition. That's how Hoffman built LinkedIn from three features to one billion users. Not planning. Thousands of iterations of move, fail, extract, adjust.

The loop compounds. And the variable that determines how much it compounds is velocity.

START VELOCITY: YOUR NEW METRIC

Most people measure outcomes: revenue, followers, results. But outcomes are lagging indicators. This means the results show up long after the actions that actually produced them. You can't control outcomes directly. You can only control whether and how fast you move. So rather than measuring outcomes, measure what I call "Start Velocity."

Start Velocity (SV) = The time between identifying an action and completing it.

There are three levels of Start Velocity: An Elite Executor has an average SV under 24 hours. An Effective Executor has an average SV under 72 hours. And stuck means an average SV over one week.

The math makes the difference concrete. If you take an average of two weeks before you act on something, that's roughly 26 shots at learning in a year. Cut that down to three days, and you're looking at around 120. That's not a small advantage; that's the difference between an executor and someone who's stuck in eternal preparing.

You track it using four data points per action: the action identified, the date identified, the date completed, and the difference. For example:

Action Identified	Date Identified	Date Completed	Start Velocity (SV)
10 prospect calls	January 5	January 7	2 days
Blog post	January 8	January 22	14 days
Workout	January 10	January 11	1 day
Average SV	—	—	5.7 days

Example Start Velocity Log

Average SV across those three: 5.7 days. Your goal: reduce that average by 20% each month.

Track this for 30 days, calculate your average, then set a goal to reduce it next month. The trend line tells you more about your trajectory than any outcome metric.

YOUR 72-HOUR CHALLENGE STARTS NOW

You've read the chapter, and you understand the system. None of that matters until you execute.

The 72-Hour loop starts the moment you close this chapter. Chapter 5 will be here when you return, and it will land differently, after you've executed your first MVA, than it would if you read it right now. Either way, keep moving.

Hour 1 (complete right now):

My Clarity Question: "I need to learn:_______________ "

Hours 2 to 12 (complete today):

My MVA: "_______________ "

Execution deadline (within 72 hours): "_______________ "

Person I'm telling: "_______________ "

Hours 12 to 72:

Execute your MVA.

Hours 72 to 73, Extraction session:

- *What I observed: "_______________ "*
- *What to do next: "_______________ "*

- *Assumption tested: "______________"*
- *Next MVA: "______________"*

THE TRUTH ABOUT EXECUTION

Goggins didn't build endurance by reading about running. He built it by lacing up his shoes at 297 pounds, making it a quarter mile, and having no idea if he'd get further the next day. Then he showed up again anyway. It taught him real lessons. Every ugly run gave him something that preparation never could: real feedback about what his body could handle, what his mind would tolerate, and what had to change before the next one. Everything that came after started with that first terrible quarter mile.

The five obstacles between understanding and doing are now named, and you know how to override each one. The 72-Hour loop is your default operating procedure. Start Velocity is your primary metric.

Pick up the phone. Take the run. Get in the pool.

Not when you're ready. Right now.

CHAPTER 4 SUMMARY

- David Goggins at 297 pounds proves the system works from any starting point. He did not succeed despite failing twice during Hell Week. He succeeded because he read failure as data and adjusted rather than quitting. He had no plan, just a question he could only answer by moving: Can I do this? The movement produced the answer.

- Five obstacles stand between understanding and doing, and all five feel like wisdom. The Illusion of Preparation is activity that avoids the external world. The Competence Trap is the belief that you must be good before you try. The Perfect Conditions Myth is waiting for circumstances that never arrive. The Confidence Requirement is waiting for a feeling that only action produces. The Research Loop is consuming information as a substitute for execution. Name the one you are in. Then take one external action.

- The 72-Hour Challenge System converts understanding into execution through four steps: identify the one question only action can answer, design the Minimum Viable Action that generates real external data, execute within 72 hours, and immediately extract the specific lesson. The loop repeats. Each cycle builds on the last.

- Start Velocity is your new primary metric. At a three-day average, you generate 120 action-feedback cycles per year. At two weeks, you generate 26. Measure it. Reduce it monthly.

WHAT'S NEXT

Chapter 5 introduces Principle 2: Identity Drives Results. You've now started executing and have a system for sustaining movement. The next question is deeper: who are you becoming through the process of executing? Because the most durable form of motivation isn't the 72-Hour loop. It's identity. When your actions align with who you believe yourself to be, execution stops feeling like discipline and starts feeling like expression.

But first, if you haven't already: execute your MVA. Chapter 5 will be here when you return.

PRINCIPLE 2:
IDENTITY DRIVES RESULTS

5. BECOME THE PERSON NOW

"Whether you think you can, or you think you can't—you're right." — Henry Ford

In the spring of 1973, Stephen King sat in the laundry room of his double-wide trailer in Hermon, Maine. He was typing on his wife Tabitha's typewriter that sat balanced on a makeshift desk wedged between a washing machine and a dryer. There was no space for a real desk. The room was just large enough for a chair, the typewriter, and a trash can.

King taught English at Hampden Academy for $6,400 a year, and Tabitha worked the second shift at Dunkin' Donuts. They had two young children, a toddler and a newborn, and barely made enough money to cover the bills. King had been writing seriously for years, selling short stories to men's magazines, and had completed multiple unpublished novels. Still, no publisher had accepted a novel yet.

That spring, he was working on a short story about a bullied teenage girl with telekinetic powers. After typing three pages, he crumpled them up and threw them in the trash because he hated the story. As he later wrote in his memoir "On Writing": "I threw it away... After all, who wanted to read a book about a poor girl with menstrual problems?"

The next morning, Tabitha emptied the wastebasket, found the crumpled pages, smoothed them out, and read them. She told him the story had promise. "You've got something here," she said. "Finish it."

King didn't believe it, but he finished the manuscript anyway.

Not because he thought it would succeed, none of his novels had been picked up by a publisher yet, but because that's just what writers do. They write.

THE DIFFERENCE

Here's what matters about Stephen King in that trailer.

He didn't wait to feel like a writer before writing each day. He didn't wait for a publisher to validate him as a writer. He didn't let years of rejection convince him he wasn't a writer. He was a writer because he wrote. Every single day, regardless of rejection, poverty, or doubt, his actions proved his identity.

Not "I want to be a writer someday." Not "I'm trying to become a writer." He wrote 2,000 words a day, including holidays and birthdays. He submitted his work despite rejection after rejection, stacking rejection letters on a spike he kept above the typewriter. He studied his craft obsessively and treated writing like a job: the same time every day, the same routine, the same goal: ten pages. His identity drove his behavior, and his behavior created his results.

THE OUTCOME

The manuscript Tabitha pulled from the trash was "Carrie." Doubleday, the largest book publisher in America at the time, accepted it in the spring of 1973, paying him a $2,500 advance. Then the paperback rights were sold to New American Library's Signet Books for $400,000. King's contractual share was $200,000, which was more than thirty times his annual teaching salary. He quit teaching and became a full-time writer.

Over the next five decades, Stephen King would publish more than 65 novels and 200 short stories, sell over 350 million copies worldwide, and become one of the most successful authors in history and became known as the "King of Horror." More than 75 of his works have been adapted for film and television, including "It", "The Shining", and "Misery." Before Doubleday said yes, approximately 30 publishers had said no.

THE IDENTITY PROBLEM EVERYONE GETS WRONG

Most people approach goals in the wrong sequence. They believe it works like this: achieve the outcome, then gain the status, then adopt the identity. For example, when I publish a book, then I'll be a writer. When I lose 50 pounds, then I'll be a healthy person. When I hit $100K in revenue, then I'll be a real business owner.

This is the outcome-first trap. You're waiting for external evidence before you'll allow yourself to become the person who creates that evidence. The issue with that logic is that it's circular. You can't get the outcome without the identity that produces it, but you won't claim the identity until you have the outcome.

The actual sequence is reversed: first, adopt the identity, then act from that identity, and then you'll generate outcomes that match.

Stephen King didn't become a writer when "Carrie" sold. He was already a writer in that trailer, with rejection letters stacked on a spike and a typewriter balanced on his knees, writing every day. "Carrie" sold because he was already a writer, and he already wrote it. He kept writing, kept submitting his manuscripts to publishers, and he kept getting rejected, until eventually a publisher accepted his manuscript. The identity came first. The outcome followed.

WHY MOST IDENTITY SHIFTS FAIL

You've tried this before. Maybe not consciously, but you've tried it. You decided to be someone who exercises, so you went out and bought the shoes, set your alarm, got a gym membership, and showed up for two weeks. Then you missed a day. Then you missed a second. Then your shoes started collecting dust, and your membership became a monthly reminder of who you're not.

You decided to be a business owner. You registered your LLC, designed your logo, and told all of your friends. Then your first sales calls went nowhere, and you started thinking: maybe I'm just not cut out for this.

You decided to be a writer. You opened the document, wrote a few paragraphs, and felt good about it. Then you reread what you'd written and thought: "Who am I kidding, I'm not a writer?"

Here's why those identity shifts collapsed: the gap between who you currently think you are and who you declared yourself to be was too large for your brain to accept.

When you're someone who hasn't exercised in three years, and you declare, "I'm an elite athlete," your brain doesn't rally behind you. It rejects the claim. Every piece of evidence in your life contradicts it. Your body contradicts it. Your history contradicts it. Your bathroom mirror contradicts it.

Psychologists call this cognitive dissonance: this is the mental discomfort of holding two contradictory beliefs simultaneously. Your brain resolves it in the easiest way available. It doesn't change your reality to match the new identity. Instead, it abandons the new identity to match your reality.

This is why affirmations fail for most people. Standing in front of a mirror saying "I am successful, I am powerful, I am unstoppable" while your bank account is overdrawn and your business has no customers doesn't build a new identity. It builds resentment toward yourself for not being the person you're pretending to be.

The identity-first approach is correct, but the execution is almost always wrong. You can't leap from who you are to who you want to become because the gap is too wide. You need to build a bridge.

THE BRIDGE IDENTITY

This is the concept that changes everything about how identity transformation actually works.

A Bridge Identity sits between your current identity and your ultimate identity, who you hope to become. It's close enough that your brain accepts it and far enough away that it drives a real identity shift. Here is what this might look like across three examples:

Fitness:

Your Current identity: "I'm someone who doesn't exercise."

Your Ultimate identity: "I'm an elite athlete."

Your Bridge Identity: "I'm someone who moves their body daily."

Why the bridge works: it doesn't require elite performance. It doesn't require believing you're athletic. It just requires that you move. One walk validates it. One set of push-ups validates it. Your brain can accept this today, and every day you validate it, the bridge extends closer toward your ultimate identity.

Business:

Your Current identity: "I'm an employee with a side hustle."

Your Ultimate identity: "I'm a successful seven-figure entrepreneur."

Your Bridge Identity: "I'm a business owner who creates value daily."

Why the bridge identity works: it acknowledges that you're building, not claiming you've already arrived. It focuses on behavior rather than outcomes. It allows for your current reality to exist while pointing it toward the future. The evidence is achievable immediately.

Writing:

Your Current identity: "I'm someone who wants to write someday."

Your Ultimate identity: "I'm a bestselling author."

Your Bridge Identity: "I'm a writer who writes daily."

This was Stephen King's actual identity in that trailer in 1973. He wasn't claiming to be a bestselling author. He was claiming to be a writer who writes, and the evidence was undeniable: 2,000 words every day, no exceptions. That Bridge Identity carried him from his laundry room to "Carrie" to 350 million copies sold. His ultimate identity formed later, built on thousands of days of evidence from his bridge identity.

The Bridge Identity solves the problem that every other approach to identity change ignores: your brain won't accept an identity it can't believe right now. But it will accept one step closer to who you want to become, if you can prove it first with daily action.

THE THREE COMPONENTS OF AN EFFECTIVE BRIDGE IDENTITY

Every effective Bridge Identity has three components. If any one is missing, the identity won't take hold.

Component 1: Present Tense

Not "I want to be" or "I'm becoming" or "I'm trying to be." It needs to be "I AM." The present tense is not a lie about where you are. It's a statement about what you're doing right now."

Component 2: Behavior-Based

Defined by actions, not outcomes. "I am someone who writes daily" is behavior-based. "I am someone who has a published book" is outcome-based.

Behavior-based identities can be validated immediately, through your own actions. Outcome-based identities require external circumstances you can't control. If you farm out your identity based on what other people do, a publisher accepting your manuscript, a customer buying your product, or your scale showing a specific weight, you've outsourced your sense of self to forces you can't control.

Component 3: Evidence-Generating

Your Bridge Identity must be provable through the daily actions you take. Every single day, you should be able to point to specific, concrete evidence that you are this person.

Bad Bridge Identity: "I am confident." How do you prove this? Confidence is a feeling, not an action. You can't log it as evidence.

Good Bridge Identity: "I am someone who takes action despite fear." This is provable. Did you take one action that made you uncomfortable today? Evidence logged.

THE SCIENCE: WHY THIS WORKS

Stanford psychologist Albert Bandura spent decades studying what he called self-efficacy: your belief in your ability to succeed in specific situations. His research revealed something that contradicts how most people think about performance.

At every level of ability, people with higher self-efficacy consistently outperform their counterparts with lower self-efficacy. Studies by Collins (1982) and Bouffard-Bouchard (1990, 1991), cited in Bandura's own later work, found that a moderately skilled person who believes they can succeed will reliably outperform a highly skilled person who doubts themselves. Belief shapes performance more powerfully than skill does.

Bandura identified four sources of self-efficacy. The most powerful connects directly to everything this book has been building toward.

Source 1: Mastery Experiences (Most Powerful)

Successfully completing challenges is what builds belief. This is the primary source, far more powerful than the other three.

King's 2,000 words per day created mastery experiences. Every day he finished his pages, his brain logged evidence: "I can write. I just proved it. Again." Those daily deposits of evidence are what built his writer identity from the inside out.

This is why your Bridge Identity must be behavior-based. Every time you complete the behavior, you create a mastery experience. Every mastery experience strengthens your identity, and the cycle compounds.

Source 2: Vicarious Experiences

Seeing similar people succeed builds belief. You think, "If they can do it, I can do it too." This is why the stories in this book matter: not because I want you to think they're impressive, but because they demonstrate that people who started from similar or worse positions built something significant through the same principles you're applying from this book.

Source 3: Social Persuasion

When people you trust tell you that you can succeed, it reinforces your belief. Tabitha telling Stephen, "You've got something here," mattered, not because it changed his manuscript, but because it reinforced his writer identity at the precise moment he was ready to abandon it. When someone else believes in you, you believe it a little more too.

Source 4: Physiological and Emotional States

When you take action despite fear, and you survive the experience, your nervous system updates its threat assessment. Your fear doesn't disappear, but its power over you diminishes because you have direct evidence that you can function in the presence of it now. Every public speaker who delivers a talk while they're terrified, then walks off stage having survived it, has just weakened their fear's influence over their next performance. Every entrepreneur who makes an uncomfortable sales call and doesn't die from the awkwardness has just made the next call slightly easier. The experience itself is the evidence. You don't need to feel fearless. You just need enough accumulated evidence that the fear no longer has the final word.

THE IDENTITY LEDGER

Knowing and understanding the Bridge Identity concept is necessary but not sufficient by itself. You need a system for building it too.

Think of your identity like a bank account. Every action you take is a transaction: either a credit toward your Bridge Identity or a debit away from it. Writing 500 words before work is a credit toward your writer identity. Skipping your writing session to doom-scroll social media instead is a debit against it.

At the end of each day, run the numbers. Credits greater than debits means you're in the black and you're moving toward your Bridge Identity. Debits greater than credits mean you're in the red, reverting back toward your old identity.

The goal is not to have a perfect ledger. You just need a positive balance over time, not a flawless record every day. If you earn five credits for your writer identity and log two debits against it, you're net plus-three for the day. Stack enough profitable days together, roughly thirty, and you'll be in the black for the month. Your identity will start to shift.

HOW KING'S IDENTITY LEDGER WORKED

Every day in that trailer, Stephen King was running his identity numbers, whether he knew it or not. On the credit side: he woke up and wrote before teaching, even when he was exhausted. He wrote his daily 2,000 words, even when he thought the writing was terrible. He submitted his manuscripts to publishers despite the ongoing rejections. He studied other published writers' books, reading constantly. He identified himself as a writer in conversations, not as an "aspiring writer." That's roughly six credits in a given day.

On the debit side: he got discouraged by rejection. He doubted his talent. He initially threw the "Carrie" manuscript in the trash. That's three debits.

Daily balance: plus-three. In the black.

Over the years before "Carrie" sold, King's identity ledger was in the black far more often than it was in the red. His ledger didn't lie. The evidence supporting his identity had accumulated, so by the time Doubleday said yes and picked up his book, King's identity was already built. The publisher didn't create Stephen King the writer. Stephen King's daily ledger did. His daily actions did. The publisher just confirmed what the evidence already proved.

THE TWO TRAPS THAT KILL BRIDGE IDENTITY FORMATION

Trap 1: Waiting to Feel Like the Identity

The mental trap: I'll start acting like a writer once I feel like a real writer. The reality: you will never feel like it until after you've done it repeatedly. Feeling follows action; it never precedes it.

This connects directly to mastery experiences: **confidence is a byproduct of action, not a prerequisite for it**. You don't need to feel like the person before you act like the person. *You execute first. The feeling follows.*

Trap 2: Letting One Bad Day Erase Twenty Good Ones

The pattern trap: you cast 20 votes in a row for your new identity. Twenty days straight of writing, training, or building. Then you miss one day. You almost instantly get discouraged and think: "See? I'm not really someone who does this because I can't do it consistently. I failed."

The reality: one missed day doesn't negate 20 successful days. You're still 20-1 in favor of your Bridge Identity. That's actually a 95% success rate.

The fix: never miss twice. Missing once is a lapse. Missing twice is the beginning of a new pattern or habit. When you miss a day, the next day becomes the most important day in your identity formation. Double down on creating your evidence. (I'll help you more with this later in the book.)

THE IDENTITY TIMELINE

Here is what you can expect as you build your Bridge Identity. Because knowing what to expect will help you identify when it might get tough so you don't quit during the phase that is inevitably going to feel difficult.

Weeks 1 to 2: The Impostor Phase.

Every action requires conscious effort, and at the beginning, you're going to feel like you shouldn't be taking those actions. The identity feels completely inauthentic, and you don't believe it yet. You feel like you're pretending. It's called "Impostor Syndrome," and it's perfectly normal. This is where everyone starts. Keep executing and keep logging your credits. Impostor Syndrome is not a signal that you made the wrong choice. It is a signal that your brain hasn't yet accumulated enough evidence to accept the new identity, which means the only thing that resolves it is the same thing you're already doing: logging credits. The feeling of being a fraud is temporary. Accumulating enough credits will make your new identity permanent.

Weeks 3 to 4: The Effortful Phase.

After you've been executing regularly, you may notice that it's taking less from you to take action. You still have to put forth effort, but slightly less than you did when you started. You're steadily building momentum. The daily credits are starting to accumulate, and you may catch yourself occasionally acting from your new identity without consciously deciding to. Keep logging your credits.

Months 2 to 3: The Automatic Phase.

Actions are starting to feel natural. You catch yourself thinking thoughts aligned with your Bridge Identity without forcing them. The behaviors that required willpower in week one now feel, simply, like what you do. Keep logging your credits.

Month 3 and Beyond: Identity Secured.

Now you ARE this person. The evidence is overwhelming, and acting from this identity feels completely natural. In fact, at this stage, not acting from it would feel strange. This is where Stephen King lived for years before "Carrie" was finally published. The identity was secured long before the outcome arrived. At this phase, you couldn't stop logging credits even if you wanted to, and you do it without thinking about it now.

A SIDE NOTE

I want to be honest with you about something.

This book is about executing before you're ready. I'm teaching you that identity has to come before the outcomes do, and I know this is true. Yet, while I was writing this chapter, I caught myself waiting to publish content until after the book was finished. The logic sounded reasonable to me at the time: finish the book first, then I'll be an author, then I'll be able to post content as an author.

I just want you to know that nobody is immune to these traps. I was waiting for external validation, a finished book, to give myself permission to act from an identity I already hold. The same outcome-first trap I just spent an entire chapter warning you about. I was standing right in the middle of it.

I'm including this because I want you to know that the gap between knowing these principles and living them is real, it's universal, and it doesn't go away. The principles in this book don't describe a state you arrive at permanently. They're describing a practice you return to every day, including the days you fall short. Especially those days.

With that out of the way, I want to address something this chapter hasn't covered yet, and it matters enormously for how you actually apply everything you just learned.

YOU AREN'T JUST ONE THING

Everything in this chapter has been about adopting a single Bridge Identity, proving it daily through your actions, and letting your identity ledger build over time. That framework is correct, but it may be incomplete for some people, because some people aren't trying to become just one thing.

You may be a father and an entrepreneur. A partner and a writer. A friend and a leader. A professional who's still figuring out what the next version of their life looks like. You're not a single identity waiting to be claimed. You're a complex person with multiple roles, multiple commitments, and multiple versions of yourself that other people depend on simultaneously.

The question isn't whether to have multiple identities. You likely already do. The question is whether they're working together or against each other, and which ones you are actually living from versus which ones you're only claiming in theory.

Psychology has studied this extensively, and what it has found is pretty compelling.

THE RESEARCH: *Patricia Linville's self-complexity theory, published in the Journal of Personality and Social Psychology (1987), found that people who hold multiple distinct role-identities are significantly more psychologically resilient than people organized around a single dominant identity. The mechanism is straightforward: when one identity takes a hit, a bad business quarter, a rejected manuscript, a professional failure, a person with a multi-identity self-concept has other sources of self-worth to absorb the blow. While a person whose entire sense of self is built around one single identity has nothing. Linville's research showed that high self-complexity correlates with lower depression, lower stress reactivity, and faster recovery from failure across populations. The protective mechanism is not complexity* *for its own sake. It's having multiple genuine, distinct sources of identity that provide independent foundations of self-worth. [5]*

Read that carefully. A single dominant identity isn't a strength. It's actually fragility dressed up as focus.

If your entire identity is based around one thing and that thing encounters some adversity and collapses, your sense of self collapses right along with it. If your entire identity is "writer" and your book gets rejected, you're not just disappointed, you're destabilized at a personal identity level. But if your identity architecture includes father, writer, entrepreneur, and community builder, a bad quarter in one domain doesn't touch the others. The foundation is distributed, it's decentralized, and no single failure can bring down the entire identity structure.

This is why the Bridge Identity system isn't about collapsing your full self into one identity. It's about deliberately building a coherent set of identities that reinforce each other, and honestly assessing which ones you are actually living from versus which ones exist only in your head.

THE IDENTITY YOU VALUE VERSUS THE IDENTITY YOU LIVE

Here is the part that is most uncomfortable to look at honestly.

You can hold multiple identities, deeply value all of them, and still only be actively living from one or two. This is the case with most people actually. The others exist as things you tell yourself matter, the things you intend to be, but they don't generate daily behavior. They're only aspirational, not operational.

Sociologist Sheldon Stryker spent decades studying how people define themselves, and the framework he built, called Identity Theory, became one of the most tested models in social psychology. He found that we all carry multiple identities at once. Parent, entrepreneur, athlete, friend. And they're not all weighed equally. Your brain ranks them based on which ones actually show up and drive your behavior in a given moment.

THE RESEARCH: Stryker (1968) established that the various identities a person holds exist in a hierarchy, with higher-ranked identities being more likely to drive behavior across situations. Stryker and Serpe (1982, 1994) then demonstrated through multiple studies that salience, how likely an identity is to generate behavior, is driven primarily by commitment: the depth and density of social networks and relationships associated with that role. A person's identities connected to strong relationships and active communities rise in the hierarchy and drive behavior consistently. A person's identities that exist only internally, with few external relationships reinforcing them, stay low in the hierarchy and rarely generate real action. Critically, Stryker and Serpe (1994) established that identity salience and identity prominence are distinct and frequently misaligned constructs. Prominence refers to how much you value an identity. Salience refers to how likely you are to actually act from it. These two rankings often don't match. [6] [7]

That last point is the one worth sitting with. What you value and what you act from are two different things. And they're frequently misaligned in ways most people never recognize.

You may deeply value your identity as a writer, a thought leader, or a public speaker. You may have held those identities for years and genuinely believed they mattered to you. But if you haven't built the relationships, commitments, and daily behaviors associated with those roles, they will stay low in your salience hierarchy. Your actions will keep defaulting to the identities that already have strong networks supporting them, the established roles with existing habits, existing communities, and daily reinforcement.

This is why people who call themselves entrepreneurs still operate, primarily, as employees. Why people who identify as writers go weeks without writing. Why people who want to be thought leaders keep waiting for the credentials that will finally make them feel legitimate before they start acting like one. The identity they want is low in the hierarchy. The identity they default to is high in it, and the gap between the two is not a motivation problem. It is a structural problem.

The gap between the identity you claim and the identity you live from is not a willpower gap. It's an architecture gap. And it won't close through intention alone.

THE GOAL IS INTEGRATION, NOT SIMPLIFICATION

Now that I've complicated the problem for you, it may feel like this is going to be harder than you thought, and you may be defaulting to a single identity, rather than identifying multiple ones. But the answer isn't to reduce your identities to one. The answer is to build what researchers call identity integration, which is a coherent architecture in where your multiple identities are consciously held, mutually reinforcing and aligned in purpose rather than competing for your time and energy.

THE RESEARCH: *A 2024 study published in the British Journal of Social Psychology (Manzi, Coen, and Regalia), drawing on a sample of 2,705 participants, found that the identity configuration associated with the highest levels of psychological well-being was not strong identification with a single role, but high identification across multiple roles combined with strong identity integration, the perception that these identities work together rather than against each other. The configuration associated with the lowest well-being was low identification across roles combined with low integration. Brook, Garcia, and Fleming (2008), publishing in Personality and Social Psychology Bulletin, confirmed the mechanism: multiple identities increase well-being when they provide similar resources and expect compatible behaviors, that is, when they reinforce each other. Multiple identities decrease well-being when they conflict, depleting resources and generating incompatible behavioral demands. [8] [9]*

In practice, integrated identities feed each other while fragmented identities compete with each other. If you're a mother, an entrepreneur, and a blogger, those identities are integrated when your entrepreneurial work is partly driven by what you want to model for your children; when your writing builds the platform that makes your business more credible; when your experience as a mother gives you the human depth that makes your content worth reading. Each identity strengthens the others. Time invested in one isn't stolen from the others.

They're fragmented when you experience them as a zero-sum competition: every hour writing is an hour not building the business, every hour on the business is an hour not being present as a mother, every hour with family is an hour not developing your platform. That experience of fragmentation isn't a scheduling problem. No calendar system fixes it. It's an identity architecture problem that requires a different solution.

The solution is to find, or deliberately build, the thread that connects them. The sentence that makes all of them make sense together. When you can articulate that, the competition between them disappears, and the identities become one coherent direction expressed in multiple domains.

HOW TO CLOSE THE GAP

You already know what drives the gap. Salience follows commitment, and commitment is built through action in the world, not through belief held privately inside your head. The research established the sequence clearly. Now the question is what to actually do with it.

The path to raising an identity's salience isn't more conviction. It's building the external structures that make the identity real to other people, and in turn, real to you. Relationships. Communities. Daily behaviors that signal the commitment outward.

THE RESEARCH: *Merolla, Serpe, Stryker, and Schultz (2012), in a study of 892 undergraduate students published in Social Psychology Quarterly, traced the complete causal chain: participation in role-relevant social structures increases commitment to an identity, commitment increases salience, salience increases behavioral intention, and follow-through. The sequence was clear and empirically supported. Stryker's broader body of work confirms that an identity existing only in a person's self-concept, without supporting social relationships or community structures, will remain low in the salience hierarchy regardless of how much the person consciously values it. Internal belief is necessary but not sufficient. External commitment is the mechanism that raises an identity from aspiration to operation. [10]*

Here is what that looks like in practice. If you want to live as a writer, the move isn't to wait until you feel like one; it's to start publishing before the book is finished. To build an audience that sees you as a writer now, before you have the finished product that feels like proof. To connect with other writers. To create the social network that raises your identity up in your hierarchy and starts generating behavior automatically, because the people around you expect it and the structures you have built demand it.

Waiting for the book to be done before publishing content is the outcome-first trap applied to identity. The book doesn't create the writer's identity. Daily writing and the community built around it do. The book is the result of an identity that was already real.

The same logic applies to every identity you value but are not yet fully living from. The question isn't "how do I believe it more?" It's:

"What relationships can I build that make this identity feel real to others and to me? What daily behavior signals this commitment to the world?" Answer those two questions and act on the answers. The identity will follow the commitment, not the other way around.

This is also how you resolve the conflict between identities that seem to compete. Two identities that feel like they are pulling against each other are usually not in conflict; they just haven't been connected yet. You aren't choosing between being a mother and being an entrepreneur. You're finding the sentence that makes both of them make sense as one single direction, then building daily structures around it. This is what integration actually means.

You can ask yourself two questions that will help you close the gap. They're simple, and they have nothing to do with belief:

What relationships can I build that make this identity real to others, not just to me?

What daily behavior signals this commitment to the world?

Answer those two questions and act on the answers. Your identity will follow your commitment.

THE IDENTITY ARCHITECTURE EXERCISE

The Bridge Identity system in this chapter gives you the tool for building a single identity. This exercise gives you the tool for understanding how all your identities fit together, and where the real gap between what you value and what you live from actually is.

It should only take about fifteen minutes, but it requires honesty, regardless of how uncomfortable it might feel.

STEP 1: LIST YOUR IDENTITIES

Write every role-identity that genuinely matters to you. Not what you think should matter, but what actually does. Father, mother, entrepreneur, writer, athlete, partner, friend, leader, creator, mentor, community member. Include all of them.

Identity 1:

____

Identity 2:

____

Identity 3:

____

Identity 4:

____

Identity 5:

____

Identity 6:

____

STEP 2: RANK BY VALUE

Rank your identities by how much they matter to you, not how you perform them, but how central they are to who you want to be. Be honest. There is no correct answer.

Most valued:

____

2nd:

____

3rd:

____

4th:

____

5th:

____

STEP 3: RANK BY SALIENCE

Now rank by behavior. Not what you value, but what your daily actions actually reflect right now. If you're unsure, look at last week's calendar. Where did your time actually go? That's your salience ranking, not what you wish it were. Which identities are generating the most consistent action? Which ones exist mostly in your intention?

Most active right now (what I actually do most):

____

2nd:

____

3rd:

____

4th:

____

5th:

____

STEP 4: EXAMINE THE GAP

Compare the two lists. Where they diverge is where the work is needed. The identities that rank high in value but low in salience are your real targets. Those are the identities you claim but aren't living from yet, not because of character failure, but because the external commitments that raise salience haven't been built yet.

Identity I value most but live from least:

____

What's missing that keeps this identity low in my hierarchy:

____

One relationship or community I could build to raise this identity's salience:

____

One daily behavior that would serve as a commitment signal for this identity:

____

STEP 5: WRITE YOUR INTEGRATION STATEMENT

Look at your top three valued identities. Write a single sentence that connects them into a coherent whole, the thread that makes all three make sense together. This isn't a mission statement. It's the sentence that resolves the competition between your identities by showing how they're actually the same direction expressed in different domains.

Example: "I am a father who is building a business and writing a book so my children grow up watching someone who executes on what they believe, not just talks about it."

My integration statement:

____

You don't need to choose between any of your identities; you need to build an architecture in which those identities feed each other instead of fighting each other. That architecture starts here.

HOW THIS CONNECTS TO EVERYTHING YOU'VE LEARNED

This is where the principles of this book begin to interlock into a single system.

Principle 1 taught you that action creates clarity. You don't think your way into a new life; you move your way into one. Now you know why that works at a deeper level. Action doesn't just produce results and feedback. Every action you take is a deposit in your Identity Ledger. Every time you move before you're ready, you log a credit for the person you're becoming and the identity you're adopting. The clarity that comes from executing isn't just informational, it's identity-forming too.

Chapter 4 gave you the 72-Hour Challenge, the system for converting ideas into action within 72 hours. Now you know the deeper purpose of that system. Every completed 72-Hour cycle isn't just generating data; it's generating evidence for your Bridge Identity. Every MVA (minimum viable action) you execute is another credit in the ledger.

As I mentioned at the beginning of this book, I use the word "execution" deliberately, rather than "action." Action is movement. Execution is deliberate, system-driven movement toward a specific outcome. Goggins didn't just move randomly; he executed against a defined goal with a measurable target and a specific feedback loop: exercise all day and keep moving. King didn't just write words; he executed a daily system with a specific output, a specific time, and a specific commitment: 2,000 words a day. When this book asks you to execute, it's asking for exactly that: not random motion, but purposeful movement with intention behind it. Keep that distinction in mind as you apply the frameworks in the chapters that follow.

Action comes first, then identity forms from sustained execution. Once identity takes hold, it drives execution automatically, without willpower, without motivation, and without forcing yourself.

Early on, you force the action, and the action builds your identity. Later, your identity drives the action, and the action strengthens the identity. But it always starts with execution. Not by standing in front of a mirror declaring who you want to be. Not with writing affirmations. Not with visualization.

Execute first. Your identity follows.

YOUR COMPLETE BRIDGE IDENTITY SYSTEM

Step 1: *Run the Identity Architecture Diagnostic (15 minutes)*

Before defining your Bridge Identity, you need to know where you are starting from. The diagnostic above maps your current identity landscape across two dimensions: how much you value each identity you hold, and how central each one is to how you see yourself day to day.

List the five to seven roles or identities that currently define you. For each one, rate two things on a scale of 1 to 5: Value (how important is this identity to who you want to become?) and Salience (how central is this identity to your daily behavior right now?)

The gap between high-value and low-salience identities is your Bridge Identity opportunity. The identity you value most but act on least is the one this chapter is designed to help you build.

My high-value, low-salience identity (the gap I am closing):

____

Step 2: Define Your Bridge Identity (5 minutes)

Complete this sentence: "I am someone who _______________"

This isn't your ultimate identity; it's your next identity, the one close enough to believe but far enough to stretch you. Three rules: it needs to be present tense (I am, not I want to be), behavior-based (defined by what you do, not what you achieve), and evidence-generating (provable through daily action).

Step 3: Identify Your Signature Behavior (5 minutes)

What is the one action that someone with your Bridge Identity does daily, without exception? Writers write. Athletes train. Business owners build. This becomes your daily identity proof, the single non-negotiable behavior that logs a credit in your ledger every time you complete it.

My Signature Behavior is: __________________

Step 4: Execute the Signature Behavior (Daily)

Every single day. Not when you feel like it. Not when you have time. Not when motivation strikes. Every day, because identity is built through repetition. One 2,000-word day didn't make Stephen King a writer. Thousands of 2,000-word days did. It doesn't need to be huge or painful, your MVA; it just needs to move you toward your ultimate identity.

Step 5: Track the Evidence (5 minutes daily)

Before bed, write down three specific pieces of evidence that you took action on, from your Bridge Identity today. For a writer identity: wrote 500 words before work (Signature Behavior), talked about your writing project with a friend (acted like a writer), read 20 pages of a craft book (learned like a writer). Whatever you did that pushed you closer to your ultimate identity, write it down.

Step 6: Review Monthly (15 minutes)

After 30 days, count the votes. How many days did you execute your Signature Behavior? How many total identity-aligned actions did you take? What is your overall ledger balance? If you hit 80% consistency or higher, your Bridge Identity is solidifying. If you didn't hit 80%, that number is still information, not a verdict. Look at which days you missed and why. Was the Signature Behavior too ambitious? Make it smaller. Was a specific trigger consistently pulling you off track? That's the next thing to address. A 60% consistency rate still means you logged evidence on more than half your days. That is more identity-building work than you were doing before you started. Keep going. Reduce the behavior until it becomes easy to execute daily, then gradually increase it. The goal is not perfection. The goal is a positive balance, maintained long enough for the identity to take hold. Once it's secured, typically by month three, you're ready to define your next Bridge Identity, one step closer to the ultimate.

YOUR COMMITMENT

My Bridge Identity is: "I am someone who

"
____

My Signature Behavior (daily identity proof) is:

"   "
____

I commit to executing this behavior daily for the next 30 days and tracking my evidence.

Signed: ______________________________

Date: ______________________________

THE TRUTH ABOUT IDENTITY

Stephen King didn't become a writer when "Carrie" sold. He was already a writer, sitting in a laundry room, on a typewriter balanced between a washing machine and a dryer, writing 2,000 words a day on his wife's typewriter, collecting rejection letters on a spike, submitting the next story before the previous rejection had time to sting.

His Bridge Identity, "I am a writer who writes daily," was so deeply embedded that throwing away a manuscript couldn't destroy it. Three crumpled pages in a wastebasket couldn't override thousands of days of evidence. Tabitha's encouragement mattered, not because it changed the quality of the work, but because it gave King one more reason to keep logging credits for an identity that was already overwhelmingly in the black.

"Carrie" didn't create Stephen King the writer.

Stephen King, the writer, created "Carrie."

That's the sequence. You don't need a publisher's permission to be a writer. You don't need a customer's payment to be a business owner. You don't need a finish line to be a runner. You claim your Bridge Identity through your actions. You prove it daily through your Signature Behavior. You track the evidence in your identity ledger, and you let the compound effect of thousands of small credits do what no single achievement ever could: make your identity permanent.

CHAPTER 5 SUMMARY

- Most identity shifts fail because the gap between who you are and who you declare yourself to be is too large for your brain to accept. Cognitive dissonance causes the brain to abandon the new identity rather than rebuild reality to match it. Affirmations fail for the same reason: they create the feeling of fraud, not the feeling of being the person.

- The Bridge Identity sits between your current identity and your ultimate identity, close enough to believe, far enough to drive change. Every effective Bridge Identity requires three components: present tense (I am, not I will be), behavior-based (defined by what you do, not what you achieve), and evidence-generating (provable through daily action). Stephen King's Bridge Identity was not "I'm a bestselling author." It was "I'm a writer who writes daily." The outcome followed the identity.

- Bandura's self-efficacy research identified four sources of belief: mastery experiences (the most powerful, actually doing the thing), vicarious experiences (seeing similar people succeed), social persuasion (trusted people confirming you can), and physiological states (surviving action despite fear and updating your threat assessment). The Bridge Identity system activates all four.

- The Identity Ledger tracks the transformation. Every action is a credit or debit. You need a positive balance over 30 days, not a perfect record. King logged far more credits than debits, and the ledger built his writer identity long before Doubleday confirmed it.

- Two traps destroy Bridge Identity formation: waiting to feel like the identity before acting (the feeling only arrives after repeated action, never before), and letting one bad day erase twenty good ones (one missed day leaves you at 20-1, a 95% success rate, never miss twice).

- The Identity Timeline shows four phases: Impostor Phase (weeks 1-2, normal, keep logging credits), Effortful Phase (weeks 3-4, momentum building), Automatic Phase (months 2-3, behavior starts running without willpower), and Identity Secured (month 3 and beyond). Every Bridge Identity follows this arc. Knowing the phases prevents quitting during the ones that are supposed to feel hard.

- The six-step Bridge Identity System runs: diagnostic first (identify your high-value, low-salience gap), then define your Bridge Identity, identify your Signature Behavior, execute it daily, track three pieces of evidence before bed, and review monthly.

WHAT'S NEXT

Chapter 6 covers Principle 3: Discipline Beats Motivation. Why the systems you build matter more than the feelings you chase, and how to execute on the days when every part of you wants to quit.

Before you turn the page, define your Bridge Identity and log your first day of evidence. Chapter 6 will land differently once you have, because by then you'll be building something, not just reading about someone who did.

SECTION 4

PRINCIPLE 3:
DISCIPLINE BEATS MOTIVATION

6. SYSTEMS OUTLAST FEELINGS

"You have power over your mind, not outside events. Realize this, and you will find strength." — Marcus Aurelius, *Meditations*

Every morning at 4:30, Jocko Willink's alarm goes off. He doesn't negotiate with it. He doesn't think about how he feels. He doesn't weigh whether today is a good day for discipline or a good day for sleeping in. The alarm sounds, and he stands up. Then he photographs his watch and posts the image online, time-stamped and dated, so there's no room for pretending. By 6:00 AM, he's finished a full workout in his garage gym. By 7:00 AM, he's deep into focused work. This has been his routine for years.

THE MAN BEHIND THE SYSTEM

Jocko Willink enlisted in the Navy at the age of 19 and spent eight years as an enlisted SEAL operator before completing Officer Candidate School and earning his commission. In 2006, during Operation Iraqi Freedom, he deployed to Ramadi as commander of SEAL Team Three's Task Unit Bruiser. While there, his unit fought in some of the most brutal urban combat American forces had seen since Vietnam.

Two of his SEALs were killed in action during that deployment. One of them was Michael Monsoor, who was a close friend. He threw himself on a grenade to save his teammates and was posthumously awarded the Medal of Honor in 2008, which is the highest military decoration awarded. Task Unit Bruiser became the most highly decorated special operations unit of the entire Iraq War. Jocko earned the Silver Star for gallantry in action and the Bronze Star for his leadership.

After twenty years of service, Jocko retired as a lieutenant commander in 2010. He co-founded Echelon Front, a leadership consulting firm. He co-authored the book "Extreme Ownership," which became a number one New York Times bestseller. He launched a podcast that has surpassed one billion downloads, and he holds a black belt in Brazilian jiu-jitsu.

Those losses in Ramadi, the friends who didn't come home, are part of what Jocko's discipline system has had to carry. The 4:30 alarm has sounded on the mornings after grief, after exhaustion, after combat, after every variety of human difficulty. The discipline wasn't designed for easy conditions. It was built precisely because conditions aren't always easy. And still, every single morning, the alarm goes off at 4:30, and he gets up. Not because he feels like it. Because the system runs regardless of his feelings.

"I wake up early and I work out every day," Jocko told Men's Journal. "Those are the minimum requirements in my life."

Not the maximum. Not mere aspirational goals. Minimum requirements. Non-negotiable actions that execute whether he's motivated, exhausted, traveling, or dealing with a crisis. Jocko has talked openly about his own battles with comfort, including a standing war with chocolate chip cookies. But perfection isn't the point. The system is. And the system runs on days when perfection is nowhere near possible.

THE WEEK-THREE WALL

By now, you've taken action. You've built your Bridge Identity. Now you're in week two, maybe week three, and something has changed.

The excitement is gone. The newness has worn off. The action that felt energizing two weeks ago now feels like a chore. You don't feel like doing it anymore.

This is exactly where most people quit. Not because they lack knowledge. Not because they don't want the results. Not because they don't believe in the goal. But because they relied on motivation, and motivation just died.

Here's what you need to understand: motivation is supposed to die. It was never designed to sustain you. It's the spark that starts the engine, not the fuel that keeps it running. If you're waiting to feel motivated before you act, you'll execute for about two weeks, then stop for the next fifty.

WHY MOTIVATION ALWAYS FAILS: THE NEUROSCIENCE

When you feel motivated, your brain is flooding you with dopamine, the same neurotransmitter that responds to food, new and exciting things, and reward. It feels powerful. It makes you feel capable of anything. The problem is that dopamine is a novelty signal, not a sustaining signal.

Researchers at Vanderbilt University demonstrated that dopamine in the nucleus accumbens, a key region of the brain's reward system, fires strongly in response to novel stimuli (new or unfamiliar experiences or objects) then decreases with repeated exposure through a process called habituation. The response fades not because the behavior becomes less valuable, but because the brain stops registering it as new. This is the same mechanism that explains why you stop noticing the texture of your clothes minutes after putting them on, or why the smell of your own home becomes invisible to you but not to visitors.

When you start a new business, a new fitness routine, or a new creative project, your brain treats it as novel. Dopamine fires. You feel incredible. You tell everyone about your new direction. You wake up excited. Then, eventually, the behavior becomes routine. Your brain re-categorizes it from new and exciting to familiar and expected. The dopamine response habituates, the feeling evaporates, and if you built your execution on that initial feeling of motivation, your execution evaporates right along with it.

This isn't a character flaw. It's neurobiology. Every human brain does this. Jocko's brain does it too. The difference is that Jocko never built his system on the feeling in the first place.

THE EVIDENCE: DISCIPLINE OUTPERFORMS EVERYTHING

If motivation is the spark and discipline is the fuel, the research is perfectly clear about which one determines outcomes.

In 2005, two University of Pennsylvania psychologists, Angela Duckworth and Martin Seligman, wanted to answer a question that most educators privately wondered about but rarely tested directly: Does being smart actually predict who succeeds and who doesn't?

They tracked 304 eighth-graders through a full school year, measuring both IQ and self-discipline. When the results came in at the end of the year, the answer was clear. Self-discipline predicted final grades, attendance, standardized test scores, and admission to competitive high schools. Smarter students were not consistently outperforming their peers. More disciplined students were. Self-discipline accounted for more than twice as much variance in academic outcomes as IQ did.

Discipline predicted success more than twice as powerfully as intelligence.

Duckworth's subsequent research expanded these findings far beyond the classroom. At West Point Military Academy, her grit scale, a psychological assessment tool that measures an individual's perseverance and passion for long-term goals, predicted which freshman cadets would survive Beast Barracks, a seven-week Cadet Basic Training, more accurately than the military's own comprehensive evaluation system, which factored in academic grades, physical fitness scores, and leadership potential ratings. Among National Spelling Bee finalists, her grit scores predicted who advanced to later rounds better than raw talent or IQ. The advantage came from one factor: grittier competitors invested significantly more hours in deliberate practice.

The pattern was the same everywhere Duckworth looked. The people who sustained effort over time outperformed the people who started with more talent, more intelligence, or more initial enthusiasm.

Discipline isn't just better than motivation. It's better than talent.

WHY THIS MATTERS MORE THAN ENVIRONMENT DESIGN

Designing your environment around your habits is valuable. Making good habits obvious and removing friction from desired behaviors genuinely helps. There's a ton of research that supports it, and entire books are written about it. But environment design has a ceiling that discipline doesn't.

You can redesign your kitchen to make healthy food visible, but when you're traveling for work and eating at airport restaurants, your environment is outside your control. You can put your running shoes by the door. But when it's cold outside, and your bed is warm, the shoes don't pull you toward them. You can put your phone in another room to reduce distraction. But your brain is still generating its own internal distractions: worry about money, doubt about the business, fear that you're wasting your time. Environment design works when you can control the environment but discipline works regardless of it.

Jocko didn't have the luxury of environmental optimization in Ramadi. There was no designing his space for success when his space was a combat zone. The discipline had to be internal, a system that ran despite conditions being actively terrible. That same principle applies to building a business, writing a book, getting in shape, or any other goal worth pursuing. Conditions won't always cooperate. The environment won't always be in your favor. You need a system that runs when the world around you isn't designed for your success.

THE DISCIPLINE OPERATING SYSTEM

The Discipline Operating System, my term for the four-component structure that makes execution automatic, isn't about white-knuckling through discomfort. It's about system design that removes the need for heroic effort every single day. Four components make execution easy and automatic.

Component 1: The Non-Negotiable Minimum Action

Jocko's minimum daily requirements are: wake up early and work out. Every day. No exceptions. No negotiations. Your system needs the same structure: one action so clearly defined that there's no question about whether or not you did it.

Define three versions of your non-negotiable action before you need any of them.

1. The full version is what you execute on normal days when conditions and motivation are both present.
2. The emergency minimum is what you execute when motivation fails, but your standard environment is fully available.

3. The contingency protocol is what you execute when your standard environment is physically unavailable, regardless of motivation.

Your contingency protocol must be designed before you need it, not during the moment you need it. When you are standing in a hotel lobby at 6 AM with a 90-minute window before a full conference day begins, you don't have cognitive resources to spare so you can design a workout from scratch.

Write your contingency protocol now: what, specifically, will you do when your standard environment is unavailable, and what are the specific situations that trigger it?

If I am traveling and my standard setup is unavailable, then I will execute [specific protocol].

Written in advance, the situation fires the response automatically. Not written in advance, the decision itself becomes the barrier, and zero becomes the likely outcome. Each version has a different trigger, and each solves a different problem. Together, these three versions mean there is no day, no circumstance, and no condition that leaves you with *zero* as the only choice. Something always exists. The system never bottoms out.

Let's say you were writing, your full version might be: write 1,000 words at your desk. Your emergency minimum might be: write one sentence at your desk when you don't feel like it, and your contingency protocol might be: write one paragraph on your phone from anywhere when your workspace is unavailable.

If you were trying to get back in shape, your full version might be: a 45-minute workout in your home gym. Your emergency minimum might be: 10 push-ups in your home gym when motivation is low. Your contingency protocol might be: push-ups and stair sprints in a hotel stairwell when you can't access a gym.

If you were working on a business, your full version might be: make 10 prospecting calls from your office. Your emergency minimum may be: make one call from your office on a low-motivation day. Your contingency protocol might be: make one outreach message sent from your phone when your office setup is unavailable.

The emergency minimum isn't about results. It's about maintaining the neural pathway. Researcher Phillippa Lally and her team at University College London tracked 96 participants over 12 weeks and found that repeated behaviors become neurologically automatic after an average of 66 days. Now, neurologically, a single missed day won't derail the rewiring, but the emergency minimum isn't just about neurology. It's also about psychology, specifically, what a missed day does to your belief that you are the person you're trying to become. One missed day is harmless to your brain's wiring. It is not harmless to your Identity Ledger. That's the science behind the emergency minimum. You're not trying to produce your best work on your worst day. You're just keeping the neural pathway alive so it can automate. One sentence on a terrible day keeps the writing pathway firing. If you do nothing, *zero* begins the process of decay.

The rule: You execute your full version when conditions are normal. You execute your emergency minimum when motivation is the only obstacle. You execute your contingency protocol when your standard environment is physically unavailable. Never neither. Never *zero*.

Component 2: The Anchor Sequence

Your brain already runs dozens of automatic sequences every day. You brush your teeth without deciding to (maybe). You pour your coffee without deliberating. You lock the door without conscious thought.

The anchor sequence attaches the new behavior to something your brain already does without effort. Instead of trying to summon motivation from scratch, you attach the new behavior to something your brain already does without thinking about it.

The formula: "After I [existing automatic behavior], I will [non-negotiable action]."

For example: "After I pour my morning coffee, I will write for 15 minutes." "After I close my laptop at 5:00 PM, I will do my workout." "After I finish lunch, I will make my prospecting calls." "After I brush my teeth at night, I will review tomorrow's priorities."

This works because it eliminates the question "when should I do this?", which is a decision point, and decision points create opportunities for avoidance. When the new behavior is anchored to an existing sequence, the existing behavior becomes the trigger, and no decision is required. The anchor fires, and the new behavior simply follows.

Run this sequence for 66 days, and the anchor will likely become permanent. It may take more time or less for you, but eventually you'll feel genuinely strange if you skip the new behavior, the same way you would feel strange leaving the house without brushing your teeth or locking your door.

Component 3: The Evidence Tracker

There's a productivity method widely known as the "Don't Break the Chain" system. The method was popularized by Jerry Seinfeld, though Seinfeld publicly disputed originating it. Regardless of who invented it, the system works, and the research explains precisely why.

Get a wall calendar. Every day you complete your non-negotiable action, mark a large X through that day. After a few days, you'll have what resembles a chain on your calendar. Your job becomes protecting that chain and ensuring that it's never broken.

Professor Benjamin Harkin of the University of Sheffield conducted a meta-analysis of 138 studies with 19,951 participants and found that monitoring progress toward a goal significantly increased the likelihood of actually achieving it. The more frequently participants monitored their progress, the greater their chance of success was.

The wall calendar does three things simultaneously: First, it creates visible evidence of your consistency. In Chapter 5, you learned that identity is built through evidence. Every X on your calendar is a tangible symbol of a deposit in your Identity Ledger. After 14 days, that chain represents two weeks of proof that you are who you say you're becoming. After 30 days, it represents a month of evidence that your Bridge Identity is real. The calendar isn't just a tracking tool. It's an identity-building machine.

Second, it creates loss aversion. After you've built a 20-day streak, breaking it would feel like destroying something valuable you've constructed. Through decades of research, behavioral economists Daniel Kahneman and Amos Tversky established that humans feel losses approximately twice as strongly as they do equivalent gains. A 20-day chain becomes psychologically expensive to break, so you're more likely to continue completing your non-negotiable minimum.

Third, it externalizes the commitment. The calendar on your wall is a standing promise, even if you're the only one who sees it. Jocko's early morning photos of his watch function the same way at scale. Your calendar doesn't need millions of witnesses though. It only needs one: you, seeing it every morning and every night.

The critical rule: if you happen to break the chain one day, never break it two days in a row. One missed day is a stumble but two missed days is the beginning of a new pattern that can derail any progress you've made. And one miss becomes permission for two. Two becomes a week. Then a week becomes "I'll start again Monday." And Monday never comes.

Component 4: The Identity Bridge Connection

This is the component that makes your Discipline Operating System different from any habit tracker or productivity method you may have tried before.

In Chapter 5, you built a Bridge Identity: an intermediate self-concept close enough to believe, but far enough to stretch you. You've been building evidence for that identity through your Identity Ledger. Now, your discipline operating system becomes the primary evidence-generating engine for that identity.

Before executing your daily non-negotiable, state your Bridge Identity and connect it to the specific action:

For example: "I am a writer who writes daily. Today I'm proving that by writing my 1,000 words."

Or "I am someone who keeps commitments to themselves. Today I'm proving that by completing my workout."

Or "I am a business builder who does difficult things. Today I'm proving that by making my sales calls."

This isn't affirmation like so much of the advice given in other books; it's a declaration followed by immediate and measurable evidence. You say who you are, and then you prove it within the next 60 seconds. The declaration without action is just meaningless words. The action without declaration is just discipline without identity. But together, they create a compounding effect: every day simultaneously builds the habit and reinforces the person you're becoming.

This is why Jocko's system works at a deeper level than just waking up early and working out. Every 4:30 AM alarm he wakes up to is evidence for his identity: a man who does what needs to be done regardless of conditions. Every photo of his watch he posts is a public deposit in his Identity Ledger. The discipline and the identity are inseparable. One feeds the other in a loop that gets stronger with every repetition.

BUILDING YOUR DISCIPLINE OPERATING SYSTEM

The entire setup should take no more than thirty minutes.

Step 1: Define Your Non-Negotiable (5 minutes)

What is the one action that, if done daily, would create the most progress toward your goal? Not ten things, just a single thing.

My non-negotiable action:

____

My emergency minimum:

____

My contingency protocol (for when my standard environment is unavailable):

____

Step 2: Set Your Anchor (3 minutes)

What is one thing you already do every single day without thinking about it?

"After I_____________________________, I will____________."

Step 3: Set Up Your Evidence Tracker (10 minutes)

Get a wall calendar or print one. Hang it where you'll see it every morning and every night. Mark today with an X if you've completed your action. If you haven't done it yet today, do it right now, then mark the X.

Step 4: Write Your Bridge Identity Declaration (2 minutes)

"I am _____________________________. Today I'm proving that by_____________________."

Write this out and place it somewhere you'll see it before you execute your non-negotiable. Next to your calendar works well.

Step 5: Design Your Environment for Zero Friction (10 minutes)

List every obstacle between you and execution. Then remove them before tomorrow.

If you're writing a book you might open your document before bed, put your phone in another room and set the coffee maker on a timer. If you're becoming more fit, you might: lay out your clothes the night before, load your workout playlist, and fill your water bottle. If you're prospecting for clients, you might pre-write your call list the evening before, block your calendar for the call window, and close any irrelevant tabs on your web browser.

Discipline = Intention − Friction.

If you reduce friction, then discipline becomes nearly effortless. This is where environment design serves discipline rather than replacing it. You're not relying on the environment to make you act. You're engineering the environment so that when your system fires, nothing stands in the way.

THE THIRTY-DAY COMMITMENT

The 30-Day Commitment below is the foundation that everything in Chapter 7 builds on. The more days of evidence you have behind you when you read it, the more it will click.

The rules:

- Execute your non-negotiable action every day

- When motivation fails, execute your emergency minimum.

- When your standard environment is unavailable, execute your contingency protocol. Never zero.

- Mark an X on your calendar every day you complete it

- State your Bridge Identity declaration before each execution

- If you break the chain, never break it two days in a row

Lally's research shows full automaticity averages 66 days, but significant formation begins around Day 21. Your brain will begin to automate. The anchor sequence will fire without conscious effort. Your identity evidence will accumulate, and the system will take hold.

Completion pledge:

"I commit to executing my non-negotiable action daily for 30 days. I understand that discipline beats motivation, and that consistency creates compound growth that motivation cannot. I commit to protecting my chain for 30 days."

Signed: _______________________________

Date: _______________________________

CHAPTER 6 SUMMARY

- Motivation is neurologically designed to disappear. Dopamine fires on novelty, then habituates as behavior becomes routine. This happens to every human brain, including Jocko Willink's. The question is never whether motivation will die. It is whether you built your system on something that outlasts it.

- Discipline does outlast it. Duckworth and Seligman's research found that self-discipline predicted academic outcomes more than twice as powerfully as IQ. The pattern held across West Point, the National Spelling Bee, and every domain they studied. Discipline is not just better than motivation. It is better than talent.

- Environment design is a valuable tool, but it has a ceiling. It works when you can control your environment. Discipline works regardless. Jocko had no environmental optimization in Ramadi. The system had to be internal.

- The Discipline Operating System makes execution automatic through four components: the Non-Negotiable Minimum in three versions (Full Version for normal days, Emergency Minimum when motivation fails, Contingency Protocol when your standard environment is unavailable, never zero); the Anchor Sequence that attaches the new behavior to something your brain already does, eliminating the decision of when to act; the Evidence Tracker, the chain calendar, that creates identity proof and loss aversion; and the Identity Bridge Connection that turns every disciplined day into proof of who you're becoming.

WHAT'S NEXT

After reading this chapter, you're executing consistently now. Your system is running, and you're marking X's on your calendar and building your unbreakable chain.

Chapter 7 will introduce the fourth Principle: Decide Fast, Adjust Faster. You've built the system that keeps you executing, now you need the decision framework that keeps you moving in the right direction, quickly and definitively.

Your chain starts today. Chapter 7 is waiting whenever you're ready, and it lands differently once you've got X's on your calendar.

PRINCIPLE 4:
DECIDE FAST, ADJUST FASTER

7. SPEED BEATS PERFECTION

"Being wrong may be less costly than you think, whereas being slow is going to be expensive for sure." — Jeff Bezos

In 1959, British industrialist Henry Kremer offered a prize of £50,000 (the equivalent of approximately $140,000 today) for the first human-powered aircraft to complete a figure-eight course around two markers half a mile apart, starting and finishing at least ten feet off the ground. The prize was considered so difficult that experts predicted it would remain unclaimed for decades. And they were right.

For eighteen years, some of the best aerospace engineers in the world attempted it. The designs they built were technically sophisticated and painstakingly constructed. And one by one, they failed. Some never achieved sustained flight, while others did but couldn't navigate the turns. The prize sat unclaimed through nearly two decades of serious engineering effort. It wasn't for a lack of talent. It was the structure of the problem itself.

Each competing team spent six months to a year designing and building their aircraft. When it crashed during testing, which happened frequently, the rebuild took another six to twelve months. At best, a team completed one or two test flights per year. Each crash was a catastrophic setback. Progress was nearly impossible because the feedback loop was so slow that by the time they learned what was wrong, an entire year had passed. Then a man named Paul MacCready looked at the problem differently.

MacCready had a PhD in aeronautics from Caltech. He was a world-record-setting glider pilot and the 1956 International Soaring Champion, the first American to win that title. He understood flight at a deep theoretical level. It should be noted that he owed $100,000 to a friend whose business had failed, and he had noticed that the Kremer Prize was worth exactly that amount at 1976 exchange rates, so he set out to win the prize.

He sat down and crunched the numbers. He calculated the relationship between wing area, total weight, and the minimum power a human could sustain over the course distance, and what he found changed everything.

Every competing design weighed two to four times more than the calculation required. The engineering community had been building aircraft strong enough to survive crashes. MacCready realized that was precisely the wrong objective. A plane strong enough to survive a crash would always be too heavy to fly efficiently. The strength and weight requirements were working directly against each other, and no one had noticed because everyone was solving the same problem the same way.

The other teams were asking: How do we build a plane that can fly this course?

MacCready asked: How do we build a plane we can repair in hours instead of months?

That single reframe was the entire competitive advantage. Not a breakthrough in materials science. Not superior engineering talent. It was a different definition of what the problem actually was.

THE DESIGN THAT CHANGED EVERYTHING

MacCready's plane was called The Gossamer Condor, and it was built almost entirely from aluminum tubing, Mylar film, and piano wire. It had a 96-foot wingspan and only weighed about 70 pounds without a pilot. When it crashed, and it crashed constantly, the team repaired it with tape and spare materials and was back in the air within hours. Sometimes they flew three or four different configurations in a single day.

MacCready began construction in August 1976. The prize-winning flight of The Gossamer Condor, piloted by cyclist and hang-glider pilot Bryan Allen, completed the Kremer course on August 23, 1977, just thirteen months after the project began.

For eighteen years, that prize lay unclaimed. MacCready won it in only thirteen months.

He didn't win because he was smarter than all of the engineers who spent eighteen years on the problem. He won because he changed the problem he was optimizing for. The other teams were optimizing each attempt, building each aircraft as strong and precise as possible before risking it in the air. MacCready was optimizing the number of attempts. He designed his plane to fail fast, to be repaired quickly, and fly again sooner.

THE PROBLEM TURNING

Midway through the project, the Gossamer Condor struggled with its turns. One day, while MacCready was on a family vacation, he watched hawks and turkey vultures soaring overhead. He timed their turns with a watch and observed how they adjusted their wing shape mid-flight, using subtle warping of the wing surface rather than rigid external control surfaces to change direction. He returned with a specific solution: adjusting the wing shape mid-flight, the same way the birds did, subtly, using the surface itself rather than bolted-on external controls. His team built and tested the modification within days.

A competitor facing the same problem would have spent weeks analyzing it, months redesigning the aircraft, months rebuilding, and then tested the revised design only once. By the time the competitor flew their corrected aircraft, MacCready would have tested fifteen variations and found exactly which one worked.

That's the compounding advantage of what I call Decision Velocity: the rate at which you complete full decision-feedback cycles. It wasn't a single decision. It was the accumulated learning from completing fifty cycles, while competitors only completed three.

THE DECISION LAYER

You built your discipline system in Chapter 6 that runs independently of how you feel and the environment you're in. That system gives you consistent execution, but consistent execution without speed creates a different problem: you can be moving forward every single day and still lose to someone who makes ten imperfect decisions in the same time it takes you to make one single careful one.

This chapter adds the speed layer. But before it can make sense, I need to define two concepts:

Execution Velocity is what happens after you commit to a course of action. It's the system, the discipline, the process that turns a decision into a result.

Decision Velocity is what happens before you commit. It's how quickly you move from identifying a choice to actually making that choice. Without decision speed, your execution system sits idle. Essentially, you'll have a high-performance engine with nobody willing to turn the key to start it.

Most people who struggle to execute aren't slow at the work itself. They're slow at deciding to start doing the work. The bottleneck isn't implementation. It's the moments before commitment, the deliberation, the research, the second-guessing, the delay.

MacCready solved both simultaneously. He built a plane that could be repaired quickly, which is execution velocity. And he made modification decisions within hours of each crash, which is decision velocity. Remove either one, and the system collapses. A team that can repair in hours but takes months to decide what to change is just as stuck as a team that decides instantly but takes months to rebuild.

THE DECISION-FEEDBACK CYCLE

Both forms of velocity only matter in the context of a complete cycle, which I call the *Decision-Feedback Cycle*. Here is what one cycle looks like from start to finish: You identify a problem or opportunity. You decide on a response. You execute it. You observe what happens. Then you use that information to decide again.

That's one cycle. MacCready completed hundreds of them in thirteen months. His competitors completed only a handful over eighteen years. The gap in outcomes wasn't the result of any single brilliant decision. It was the accumulated learning from running far more cycles.

This is what decision velocity actually measures: not how fast you make any individual decision, but the rate at which you complete full cycles. And, as with any form of compounding, the advantage grows over time. Faster cycles generate more data, better data produces better decisions, and better decisions speed up the next cycle.

The person who completes fifty cycles in a year doesn't just beat the person who completes six. They beat them by a margin that widens every month the gap continues to grow.

WHAT SLOW DECISIONS ACTUALLY COST YOU

The most common story people tell themselves about slow decision-making is that they are being thorough. That they're being careful or responsible. They are gathering more information so they can make an informed decision. And that story has a cost that rarely gets calculated.

Lost momentum is the first cost. The energy and clarity present at the moment a decision surfaces, are highest at that very moment. Every day you delay, the window narrows, the specificity of what you wanted to do blurs, and other priorities fill the space.

Compound delays follow from lost momentum. One slow decision creates downstream waiting: the vendor waiting for your approval, the team waiting for direction, the opportunity that closes while you deliberate. Slow decisions don't just cost you the day you spend deciding. They cost you everything downstream.

Opportunity cost of learning is MacCready's insight applied directly to your life. Every decision you delay is a cycle you don't complete. The person who makes ten imperfect decisions and adjusts is learning from ten different datasets. You're learning from zero while you sit around and deliberate.

Decision debt accumulates on top of all of it. Undecided questions don't disappear. They stack as background cognitive load, consuming processing resources while producing absolutely nothing.

Eroded self-trust is the final cost, and sometimes the most damaging. Every time you tell yourself you'll decide and then you don't, you teach yourself that your commitments to yourself are unreliable. Over time, the mere act of facing a decision triggers avoidance, because your history says you won't follow through anyway.

None of these costs is visible at the moment of delay. They accumulate invisibly. That's why slow decision-making feels safe but actually isn't.

THE SCIENCE: WHY FASTER CYCLES ALWAYS BEAT SLOWER ONES

The conventional assumption is that more information produces better decisions. The research consistently shows that this is true only up to a point.

Iyengar and Lepper's study, which appeared in Chapter 1 in the context of research loops, reveals the same mechanism at work in decision-making: beyond a certain threshold, additional options do not improve decisions. They prevent them.

The structural reason is straightforward. Your capacity for analysis is finite. Every additional variable you consider beyond the threshold that would have been sufficient consumes cognitive resources without improving the output. The mental energy spent processing marginal differences between options is energy that isn't available for executing the decision you should have already made.

Stanford professor Kathleen Eisenhardt's landmark 1989 study of eight technology firms in high-velocity competitive environments found that fast-deciding executive teams outperformed slow-deciding ones across every performance measure. Counterintuitively, the fast decision-makers also used more information, not less, and developed more alternatives. Their advantage wasn't in cutting corners. It was in processing information efficiently and moving before the opportunity changed. The slower teams weren't more thorough. They were simply slower, and the market punished them for it.

MacCready's design solved this problem at the engineering level. By building a plane he could repair in hours, he compressed each cycle so tightly that he never accumulated enough uncertainty to be paralyzed. He always had recent data. He was always moving. His decision about what to change next was never a long deliberation because the evidence from the last flight was fresh, and he was already prepairing the next flight.

THE 70% RULE

In his 2015 letter to Amazon shareholders, Jeff Bezos (Amazon's founder) introduced a framework that became foundational to Amazon's operating culture: the distinction between one-way door decisions and two-way door decisions. One-way doors are consequential and difficult or impossible to reverse. Two-way doors are reversible. You can walk back through if the outcome isn't what you wanted.

Bezos observed that the most damaging tendency in large organizations is treating two-way door decisions with one-way door caution. Teams spend weeks deliberating over pricing changes the way they should deliberate over selling the company. They apply slow, consensus-heavy processes to decisions that could be tested and reversed in a week. The result, in Bezos's framing, is slowness, unthoughtful risk aversion, and diminished innovation.

His rule for two-way door decisions: decide fast and be prepared to correct quickly. His rule for one-way door decisions: slow down, gather more information, and get it right. The single question before any significant decision is: "Can I walk back through this door if I am wrong?" If yes, speed matters more than certainty. If the answer is no, take more time.

In his 2016 letter, Bezos named the specific threshold: most decisions should probably be made with around 70% of the information you wish you had. If you wait for 90%, in most cases, you are probably being slow. He then completed the thought in a way that most summaries of this framework leave out, and it is the most important part: being good at course correcting changes the math entirely. If you can correct quickly when you are wrong, then being wrong is far less costly than it appears. But being slow is always expensive, regardless of whether the eventual decision is right or not.

This is the complete framework, not just the speed threshold. The 70% threshold only makes sense in the context of the reversibility test that precedes it and the course-correction capacity that follows it. They are three parts of the same system.

THE SEQUENCE

First, you need to know: Is this a one-way door or a two-way door? If it is a one-way door, you can take more time. If it is a two-way door, move to the 70% Check.

Second: Do you have roughly 70% of the information you need? It's not a precise calculation, but a genuine gut check: have you gathered the core information that would materially change your decision? If yes, make the decision. If you're still missing something fundamental, identify specifically what it is and how long it might take to get it. If the answer is more than a week, the missing information probably won't improve your decision enough to justify the delay.

Third: Are you prepared to correct course quickly if the decision turns out to be wrong? If the answer is yes, then being wrong is recoverable. Decide and execute.

The 70% figure is a heuristic, not a measurement. You probably can't calculate it precisely. What it identifies is the point at which continued research produces diminishing returns. Most people have a reliable intuition for when they have reached it and choose to keep researching anyway, because more research feels productive, and deciding feels risky. The framework is a permission structure to execute on what you already know.

DECISION VELOCITY: THE FORMULA

All of this comes together into a single, measurable concept.

Decision Velocity = Cycles Completed per Unit of Time

A cycle is: identify a decision, make it, execute it, observe the result, then use that information to decide again. One complete loop.

Velocity is how many complete loops you finish in a given period. MacCready completed hundreds in thirteen months. His competitors completed a handful in eighteen years.

Two variables determine your velocity. The first is how quickly you move through the deciding and executing phases of each cycle. The second is whether your decisions are reversible enough to let you enter the next cycle quickly when the outcome isn't what you expected. One-way door decisions that go wrong can end your cycle entirely. Two-way door decisions that go wrong just begin the next cycle with better information.

This is why the door framework and the 70% threshold are not two separate ideas. They are two inputs into the same equation. The door test tells you how much a wrong decision will cost you. The threshold tells you how much certainty you need before you can afford to find out. Together, they determine how fast your cycles can run.

THE MATH OF DECISION VELOCITY

Consider two people facing the same situation for one year.

Person A waits for 90% certainty before deciding. Each decision takes four to eight weeks of analysis. They complete approximately six full cycles over the year.

Person B decides at 70% confidence on two-way door decisions. Each cycle takes three to seven days. They complete approximately fifty full cycles over the year.

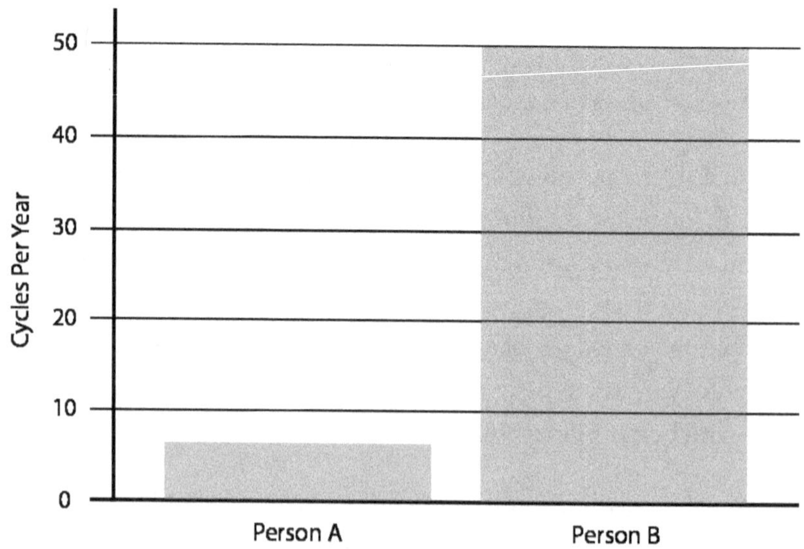

At the end of the year, Person A has six data points and is still seeking certainty on the next decision. Person B has fifty data points and has adjusted based on each one. Their judgment is sharper, their process is faster, and the gap between them widens with every additional cycle.

Person B didn't have better information. They just had more feedback loops, which gave them more real data points. That's the compounding advantage of decision velocity.

BUILDING YOUR DECISION VELOCITY

Decision velocity is a muscle you can build. Here's how to build it without starting a separate practice from scratch.

You should already have your Evidence Tracker running from Chapter 6, the chain calendar where you mark an X for every day you execute. Just add one column to it. Every day, when you log your execution, also log the most significant decision you faced and how long it took you to make it. That's it. No new journal. No new habit. One additional data point alongside the tracking you are already doing.

At the end of the first week, count how many decisions you deferred beyond 48 hours. That's your baseline.

From that point forward, apply the following sequence to every decision you encounter:

Step One: The Door Test

Before anything else, ask yourself one question: "Can I reverse or significantly adjust this decision within 30 to 90 days if it turns out to be wrong?"

If yes, it is a two-way door. Decide within 48 hours using at least 70% confidence.

If no, it's a one-way door. Take more time, but set a hard deadline in advance. Even one-way doors need a decision date. Open-ended deliberation on irreversible decisions is how careers and businesses stall.

Step Two: The 70% Check

For two-way door decisions, ask yourself honestly: have I gathered the information that would materially change my decision if I had it? Not all possible information. Just the information that matters.

If you've already gathered that core information, you're at 70%. Decide now.

If you're missing something specific and fundamental, identify exactly what it is and how long it would realistically take to get it. If the answer is more than a week, the missing information is almost certainly not going to change your decision enough to justify the wait. Decide with what you have.

Step Three: Track Your Velocity

Each week, review your decision log from the previous seven days.

Count: how many two-way door decisions did you resolve within 48 hours? Compare that number to your baseline from Week 1. Your target isn't a fixed percentage. Your target is simply measurably faster than where you started, sustained over time. A person who moves from resolving 20% of decisions within 48 hours to resolving 40% has made more meaningful progress than someone who moves from 75% to 81%, regardless of which number looks better on paper.

Track this weekly for eight weeks. Watch what happens to your momentum and to the quality of your outcomes. Not every fast decision will be correct. Some will need to be corrected. That's built into the system. What you'll notice is more learning cycles completed, less background cognitive weight from undecided questions, and a growing confidence in your own judgment that only comes from repeatedly trusting it.

WHEN THE SYSTEM FAILS

Deciding faster will surface a fear that slower decision-making was quietly suppressing: the fear of being wrong.

When you decided slowly, being wrong felt like a failure of the process. You gathered enough information and still got it wrong. That's demoralizing. When you decide at 70% confidence, being wrong is sort of an expected outcome built into the design. That's a fundamentally different relationship with mistakes, and it takes time to internalize.

The failure mode to watch for is not bad decisions. It's the impulse to slow back down after a decision turns out to be wrong. The discomfort of being wrong at 70% is designed to be temporary, because the system assumes you'll correct quickly. If you correct quickly, the wrong decision costs you a cycle. If you react to being wrong by returning to the 90% waiting pattern, you pay for the wrong decision and lose all the velocity you were building.

Being wrong faster is only an advantage if you also correct faster. And that's what the next chapter is going to show you.

CHAPTER 7 SUMMARY

- Paul MacCready won in thirteen months what eighteen years of careful engineering could not. He did not have better talent. He changed what he was optimizing for. Every other team was optimizing each aircraft. MacCready was optimizing the number of attempts. The Gossamer Condor was built to fail fast, repair fast, and fly again.
- Slow decisions carry five compounding costs: lost momentum (clarity is highest at the moment a decision surfaces and decays with every day of delay), compound delays downstream (vendors, teams, and opportunities all wait), opportunity cost of learning (every delayed cycle is a dataset you never generate), decision debt (unresolved questions consume cognitive load while producing nothing), and eroded self-trust (every unkept commitment to yourself makes the next one harder to keep).
- Decision Velocity is the rate at which you complete full decision-feedback cycles, not how fast you make any individual decision. It compounds. Faster cycles generate better data. Better data produces better decisions. Better decisions speed up the next cycle. Person A, with 90% certainty, completes six cycles per year. Person B at 70% confidence completes fifty. The gap widens every month.

- Decision Velocity and Execution Velocity are distinct. Decision Velocity is what happens before you commit, how quickly you move from identifying a choice to making it. Execution Velocity is what happens after, how efficiently your system turns the decision into a result. Both are required. Fast decisions without execution create nothing. Fast execution without decisions never starts.

- The Bezos framework is three parts, not one: assess reversibility first (one-way door decisions warrant deliberation; two-way door decisions warrant speed), decide at 70% for reversible decisions (the last 30% rarely changes the outcome and always costs time), and be ready to correct course quickly (being wrong at 70% is recoverable; being slow is expensive regardless). Build velocity by adding one column to your Evidence Tracker, log each decision, and how long it took. Establish your baseline. Reduce it monthly.

WHAT'S NEXT

You can now decide faster. But deciding faster means you will also be wrong more often than someone who waits for 90% certainty. That's intentional. And the question isn't how to avoid being wrong. It's how to correct course fast enough that being wrong becomes an advantage rather than a cost.

Chapter 8 addresses the most dangerous phase of execution, the gap between your inputs and your visible results. You will be deciding faster and executing consistently. The question Chapter 8 answers is: how do you keep going when the results you expect haven't arrived yet?

Before you go there: add the decision column to your existing tracking system today. One column. One question. Log it every day this week and establish your baseline. That number is what Chapter 8 will build on.

SECTION 6

PRINCIPLE 5:
TRUST THE INVISIBLE WORK

8. TRUST THE INVISIBLE WORK

"The two most powerful warriors are patience and time." — Leo Tolstoy, War and Peace

In 1883, a 31-year-old architect named Antoni Gaudí took over a struggling construction project in Barcelona. The original architect had resigned after disagreements over materials. The project was a church, funded entirely by private donations, with no guaranteed timeline, no government support, and no completion date. Gaudí accepted it.

He worked on the Sagrada Familia for 43 years. From 1914 onward, he stopped taking other commissions and devoted himself exclusively to it. He eventually moved onto the construction site. When asked why the project was progressing so slowly, he is reported to have said: "My client is not in a hurry."

By the time he was struck and killed by a streetcar in 1926, only one tower of the Nativity facade had been completed, and less than a quarter of the structure stood. Bystanders who found him initially mistook him for a beggar. He had stopped caring about his appearance. The building was everything.

In 1936, during the Spanish Civil War, anarchists set fire to the crypt and destroyed the workshop where Gaudí had stored all of his plaster models and original plans. Most were lost. The architects who followed him spent decades reconstructing his designs from photographs, fragments, and surviving calculations. Computer-aided design, introduced in the 1980s, finally allowed accurate execution of his complex geometries. Construction passed the midpoint in 2010. Pope Benedict XVI consecrated the building that year.

Construction of the church began in 1882, and as of 2026, the central Tower of Jesus Christ is being completed, and the Sagrada Família became the tallest church in the world on October 30, 2025, at 162.91 meters. It has taken 144 years.

Every stone Gaudí placed between 1883 and 1926 is still holding up the structure today. Every engineering solution he modeled before his death, even the ones destroyed in the Civil War and reconstructed from fragments, is embedded in what stands. He was not placing stones for a building he would see finished. He was placing stones because they were the correct stones to place, and the arch could not stand without them.

You are placing stones right now. But you may not be able to see the arch yet. That is not evidence of failure. That's the correct sequence for building anything.

THE EVIDENCE GAP

The problem with putting work into anything is that you see your effort immediately. You log the session. You write the words. You make the calls. You consistently show up. The effort is visible to you the moment it happens.

The problem is that you only see evidence of the product of that effort much later. The body that builds more muscle. The skill that becomes fluent. The business that starts generating significant revenue. The audience that finds your content. These are delayed returns on investments you made when no one was watching and when no one was noticing, including yourself.

The gap between effort and the product of your efforts is what I call the *Evidence Gap*. And it's where most people quit. Not because the effort isn't working, but because they can't see it working, and the absence of visible results looks identical to failure.

This isn't a problem with motivation. It's a timeline problem. The person who quits at month six hasn't given up on the goal. They've made a reasonable assumption from incomplete information: six months of consistent effort with no visible outcome is reasonable evidence that the approach isn't working. The assumption is absolutely wrong, but the reasoning is rational, given what they can see.

The Evidence Gap exists in every domain of meaningful growth, and if you don't understand it, you will quit during it, thinking the system failed, when in reality the system was working the entire time.

EVIDENCE IS ALWAYS THE LAST THING TO ARRIVE

This pattern isn't unique to human effort. It is built into how nature, science, and systems work at every scale.

Consider a seed. When you plant it, it absorbs water and activates a metabolic process entirely underground. The embryonic root, called the radicle, grows downward first, anchoring the plant and absorbing nutrients before anything breaks the soil surface. By the time you see the first sprout, a root system is already established below. The visible growth is the last thing that happens, not the first. If you dug up the seed on day three because nothing had appeared above ground, you would destroy a system that was already working.

A hurricane begins as a tropical wave off the coast: a loose cluster of thunderstorms over warm water with no visible structure. It progresses through four stages, gathering energy from warm ocean water the entire time, building its internal rotation and pressure systems over days and sometimes weeks. By the time it has a name and makes the news, the invisible accumulation of energy has been underway for a very long time. No one reports on a tropical disturbance. Everyone reports on the hurricane. But the hurricane was being built while no one could see it.

Consider compound interest. Warren Buffett started investing at age 11. He became a billionaire at 56. But 95 percent of his net worth was accumulated after age 65, on a compound foundation he spent 54 years building. The first 54 years built the base, but the compounding became visible in the final decades. His skill didn't change in his sixties. The compound base simply became large enough for the massive returns to show.

Seeds, storms, compound returns. The structure is identical every time: invisible inputs accumulate below the surface, and the visible output appears only after the invisible work crosses a threshold. The delay between input and output varies. The structure doesn't.

WHY THE GAP EXISTS

The Evidence Gap is not a design flaw in how growth works. It's the mechanism.

In Chapter 7, you learned that habits become neurologically automatic in an average of 66 days. That's when the behavior stops requiring conscious effort. But the results of that behavior take longer to appear, because results are the compound output of many repeated behaviors over time, not the output of any single one. The behavior automating and the results appearing are two different events happening on two very different timelines.

This is supported by research on skill acquisition. Fitts and Posner's three-stage model of learning, one of the most widely cited frameworks in cognitive science, shows that skill development follows a predictable pattern. First, a cognitive stage where you learn the basics and think through every step. Second, an associative stage where you begin combining parts of the skill and eliminating major errors. Third, an autonomous stage where execution becomes partially automatic, and you can focus on higher-level refinement. The transition from the first stage to the third is not linear. There are plateaus where visible progress stalls, even though neurological adaptation is continuing through all of it beneath the surface.

This is the Evidence Gap in action. The inputs are real. The progress is real. The evidence is delayed.

YOUR TIMELINE IS WRONG (AND THAT'S NORMAL)

Here is where it gets dangerous.

Most people don't just underestimate how long results take to appear. They systematically underestimate it, and they do so in a predictable and well-documented way.

Daniel Kahneman and Amos Tversky identified this phenomenon as the *planning fallacy*. Their research, published across multiple studies and later synthesized in Kahneman's book Thinking, Fast and Slow, showed that people consistently underestimate the time, costs, and risks of future actions while overestimating their benefits. This isn't a character flaw. It is a cognitive bias that affects virtually everyone, from individual goal-setters to large organizations managing billion-dollar construction projects.

The planning fallacy compounds in domains where feedback is delayed. When you can't see progress, you tend to assume you're further along than you are, which generates premature expectations of results that the timeline cannot yet deliver.

This is why I recommend what I call the Invisible Multiplier Rule: Whatever timeline you currently believe your goal requires, extend it significantly, 2 - 2.5 times. Not because you are pessimistic, but because the planning fallacy is reliable and universal. Build in surplus. Surplus gives you room to stay in. Deficit, on the other hand, gives you a deadline to quit against. If you think your business will generate meaningful revenue in six months, plan for twelve to fifteen. If you think your fitness transformation will be visible in three months, plan for six to eight. If you think your content will find an audience in six months, plan for twelve to eighteen.

This is not pessimism. It is calibration. When you plan for fifteen months, and results appear at month twelve, you have a surplus, and you feel great about it. When you plan for six months, and results don't appear until month twelve, you have already quit at month seven because you were past your expected date with nothing to show.

Gaudí didn't plan to be unknown for four decades. But he didn't quit at year ten when the recognition had not arrived. His arch eventually appeared, and it will for you too, provided you're placing the right stones in the right places.

THE RIGHT STONES: A DIAGNOSTIC FRAMEWORK

Everything in this chapter assumes one critical condition: that you are executing the right process. If you are doing the right things consistently, the results will come. The Evidence Gap is structural and temporary. But if you are doing the wrong things consistently, no amount of patience will produce the result you want.

This distinction matters more than anything else in the chapter. Patience applied to a broken process is not persistence. It's stubbornness. "Just keep going" is dangerous advice if the path is wrong.

So how do you know? How do you distinguish between the Evidence Gap, where the process is working but the results haven't surfaced yet, and a genuinely broken approach that needs correction?

Here are five diagnostic questions. If you can answer yes to three or more of these, you're likely in the Evidence Gap. If you can't, the issue may not be patience. It may be the process.

1. **Is someone ahead of you succeeding with a similar approach?** If others have achieved what you want using the same general method, the method works. You are earlier in the

timeline. If no one has ever succeeded this way, that is a different problem.

2. **Are your inputs improving in quality?** Even when results are invisible, your execution should be getting sharper. Your writing should be better at month six than it was at month one. Your sales conversations should be more precise. Your workouts should be more focused. If the quality of your inputs is flat or declining, the system needs adjustment, not more time.

3. **Are you getting micro-feedback even without macro-results?** Micro-feedback is the small signals that the work is landing. A prospect who says no but engages longer than last month's prospect. A reader who shares one of your posts even though your overall following hasn't grown. A personal record in the gym, even though your body composition hasn't visibly changed. Micro-feedback means the system is producing output. It just hasn't compounded to the visible threshold yet.

4. **Can you explain why it should work?** Not just that you believe it will work. Can you articulate the mechanism? If your business model has a clear path from input to revenue, and you are executing on that path, you're likely in the Evidence Gap. If you can't explain how your current actions connect to the result you want, you may be busy without being effective.

5. **Has a knowledgeable person reviewed your approach?** Not a friend who supports you emotionally. A person with relevant expertise who can evaluate your method. If someone who has done what you're trying to do looks at your approach and says the inputs are correct, trust the process. If you have never had your approach evaluated by someone qualified, that is the first stone to place.

If you answered yes to most of these, you're in the Evidence Gap. Keep placing your stones. If you answered no to most of these, the chapter you need right now isn't this one. Return to Chapters 3 and 4 and recalibrate your approach before investing more time in a system that may not be pointed at the right target.

THE FIVE PSYCHOLOGICAL STAGES OF THE EVIDENCE GAP

Even when the process is right, the Evidence Gap is emotionally brutal. Understanding where you are in it doesn't eliminate the difficulty, but it does remove the misdiagnosis. When you know the stage you're in, you stop interpreting a normal phase as personal failure.

Stage 1: Initial Momentum. The system is new. Execution feels energized. You're building habits, installing systems, and making decisions. You feel forward motion. This is real, but it's partly driven by novelty. Stage 1 isn't representative of what the work will feel like long-term.

Stage 2: Doubt Emerges. The novelty has faded. The discipline system is no longer new. Results haven't appeared. The voice that says "this isn't working" makes its first appearance here. This is normal. Stage 2 doesn't mean the system is failing. It means the system is becoming real work rather than exciting new work. Your response to Stage 2 determines everything downstream.

Stage 3: The Grind. This is the floor of the Evidence Gap. Input is consistent, but evidence is minimal or absent. External validation is low. The system requires you to trust the process rather than the outcomes. This is where most people exit. The ones who don't are building the foundation that Stage 4 will stand on.

If you're reading this and recognizing yourself in Stage 3, you are in the correct place doing the correct things at the correct time. You aren't behind. You're in the expected phase of a working system. Stage 4 exists. You just can't see it from here.

Stage 4: The Breakthrough Zone. This is when compound returns begin to surface. Not all at once, it shows up in accelerating increments. What felt like grinding in Stage 3 begins to produce visible output. The systems you installed earlier are now becoming automatic. The inputs from Stage 3 are generating returns that appear sudden to outside observers but were entirely predictable from inside the process.

Stage 5: The Compound Phase. Each month builds on all previous months. The same inputs now produce larger and larger outputs because the compound base has grown. This is when Gaudí's arch became visible. This is when Buffett's net worth exploded. This is when everything that happened in the invisible years appears, compressed, as an overnight success to everyone who only started watching at Stage 5.

THE 90-DAY INVISIBLE WORK COMMITMENT

This commitment runs concurrently with your discipline practice from Chapters 6 and 7. You're not adding a new behavior. You are adding a tracking framework to the behaviors you have already installed, and you're committing to measure inputs rather than outcomes for the next 90 days.

> *I commit to executing my system for 90 days, targeting your non-negotiable minimum every day (your full execution, emergency minimum & contingency protocol from Chapter 6), with*

a target execution rate of 95 percent or higher, never missing two consecutive days.

I commit to tracking inputs only. Did I execute today? Hours invested. One lesson learned. Not: what result did I produce?

I commit to not evaluating outcomes until Day 91. I will not assess whether the system is working based on visible results before the 90-day input period is complete.

I acknowledge: I am likely in Stage 2 or Stage 3 right now. That is the correct stage. The evidence is underground. The arch is not yet visible. I am placing stones.

My domain:

____

My realistic timeline (current estimate extended by the Invisible Multiplier):

____

My current stage (1 through 5):

____

My input metric for the next 90 days:

____

Gaudí spent 43 years placing stones for a building that wouldn't be fully complete until 144 years after construction began. By the time he died, bystanders mistook him for a beggar. He had given everything to a project whose visible results wouldn't arrive during his lifetime. Every stone he installed though, still holds the structure in place today.

Warren Buffett spent 54 years building a compound base before 95 percent of his wealth became visible. His skill didn't change. Time did.

A seed builds its root system in darkness before the sprout breaks the surface. A storm gathers its energy for days over open water before it has a name. You aren't behind. You're in the Evidence Gap. And The Evidence Gap isn't failure. It's the structural requirement of any goal worth pursuing. The gap between your effort and your evidence isn't evidence of a broken system. It's evidence of a working system that has not yet reached the threshold where its outputs become visible to you.

Results lag and inputs compound. The Evidence Gap between them isn't the problem. It's the process.

CHAPTER 8 SUMMARY

- The Evidence Gap is structural, not personal, and it is where most people quit. You see your effort immediately. You see evidence of that effort much later. The gap between them is not a sign that the system is broken. It is the mechanism through which every meaningful result is built. Seeds, storms, compound returns, the structure is identical every time: invisible inputs accumulate below the surface, and the visible output appears only after the invisible work crosses a threshold.

- Fitts and Posner's skill acquisition model confirms why: development moves through cognitive, associative, and autonomous stages. Progress plateaus between stages even as neurological adaptation continues underneath. The behavior automating and the results appearing are two different events on two different timelines.

- Your timeline is almost certainly wrong, not because you are pessimistic, but because the planning fallacy is universal and well-documented. Apply the Invisible Multiplier Rule: extend your current estimate by two to two-and-a-half times. Surplus keeps you in. Deficit gives you a deadline to quit against.

- Before attributing slow results to the Evidence Gap, verify the process with five diagnostic questions: Is someone ahead of you succeeding this way? Are your inputs improving in quality? Are you getting micro-feedback? Can you explain the mechanism connecting your actions to your result? Has a knowledgeable person reviewed your approach? Three or more yes answers mean you are in the Evidence Gap. Keep placing stones. Mostly no answers means the issue is the process, not the timeline. Return to Chapters 3 and 4 and re-calibrate.

- The five psychological stages map the emotional terrain. Stage 1 (Initial Momentum) is novelty-driven, real but not representative. Stage 2 (Doubt Emerges) is when the voice that says "this isn't working" arrives for the first time, your response here determines everything downstream. Stage 3 (The Grind) is the floor of the Evidence Gap, where most people exit. If you recognize yourself here, you are in the correct place, doing the correct things at the correct time. Stage 4 (The Breakthrough Zone) is when compound returns begin surfacing in accelerating increments. Stage 5 (The Compound Phase) is when the same inputs produce larger and larger outputs because the compound base has grown.

WHAT'S NEXT

You now understand that the Evidence Gap is structural, not personal. You have a diagnostic framework for distinguishing between invisible progress and a broken process, and a commitment to measure inputs rather than obsess over outputs.

But there is a practical problem this chapter doesn't fully solve: knowing intellectually that the gap exists doesn't make living through it easy. Month 6, no visible results, external skeptics asking questions, financial pressure building, the voice saying quit louder every week. Understanding the Evidence Gap does not silence any of that. It just means you know what is happening. Knowing doesn't automatically change how you respond.

The next chapter provides the operational systems for staying in during the grind phase: how to track invisible progress in ways that generate real evidence the work is happening, how to build external accountability structures that persist through Stage 3, and how to handle the specific conversations that derail execution, including the friend who asks when you are going back to a real job, the family member who says it's not working, and the internal voice that has the same question every morning: "Is this working? Am I wasting my time?"

9. MEASURE WHAT MATTERS NOW

"Don't let what you cannot do interfere with what you can do." — Coach John Wooden

Chapter 8 established that the Evidence Gap is structural. This chapter gives you the operational systems for executing through it.

Intellectual understanding of the Evidence Gap and emotional resilience during the Evidence Gap are two different skills. Chapter 8 gave you the first. This chapter gives you the second. Specifically, it gives you three things: a system for tracking what you can actually control, a method for collecting evidence of underground progress that would otherwise go unnoticed, and three strategies for persisting through the gap when everything inside you says to quit.

TRACKING INPUTS, NOT OUTPUTS

Here is how most people measure progress during the Evidence Gap. They check their follower count. They look at their revenue. They step on the scale. They count the pages they have written. They refresh the inbox. These are output metrics; they measure results that have already occurred or have not yet arrived. They're lagging indicators, meaning they only tell you what has already happened, not what's currently building.

Focus on output metrics during the Evidence Gap produces one result: despair. Not because the outputs are bad, but because they just haven't surfaced yet, Chapter 8 established that. The outputs are underground. So measuring them each day during the gap is equivalent to digging up a planted seed every morning to check whether it's sprouted yet. The checking itself disrupts the process and only confirms your fear.

Executors, people who apply the principles in this book, don't measure outputs daily. They measure inputs. They track what they showed up and did, not what the world has done in response to it. This distinction is the difference between measuring something you control and measuring something you don't.

Executors track inputs they can control. Everyone else tracks outputs they cannot.

THE CONTROL PRINCIPLE

You control whether you execute your system today, but you can't control when your audience finds your YouTube channel, when your retail business turns inventory, or when the skill finally clicks. Those outcomes are affected by your inputs, but they are not determined by them. They operate on a delayed timeline that is structurally beyond your control.

Frustration during the Evidence Gap is almost always frustration with something you can't control: the results haven't appeared yet.

Redirecting attention to what you can control removes the frustration with the uncontrollable and replaces it with something useful, evidence that you're doing the work, which is the only thing that actually matters.

You showed up today. That is something you controlled. You cannot control whether it produces a visible result by tomorrow, but you can control whether you show up tomorrow.

THE PROCESS METRICS SYSTEM

The Process Metrics System is a simple system that has three levels, and each level builds on the previous. Together, they give you a complete picture of your input activity without requiring you to obsess over outputs that haven't arrived yet.

Daily Tracking (three data points)

Did I execute today (full execution, emergency minimum, or contingency protocol from Chapter 6)? Y / N

Hours invested: _______

One   thing   I   learned   or   adjusted:

____

That's it. Three data points. No outcome assessment. No checking revenue, followers, or scale. Those are output metrics, and they are not part of daily tracking. You're not in the output phase yet. You are in the input phase.

Weekly Tracking (five data points, Sunday evening)

Days executed this week: ___ / 7

Total hours invested: ______

System working? Y / N

One   thing   to   adjust   next   week:

____

One   piece   of   evidence   collected:

____

Monthly Tracking (one comprehensive review, last day of each month)

Total execution days this month: ___ / 30

Total hours invested: ______

Is the current system working? Y / N

Adjustment needed: ____

After reviewing your inputs and confirming you have been executing consistently, check your output metrics once per month, but only after the input review is complete. Monthly output checking is fundamentally different from daily output checking. You are consulting a lagging indicator after confirming your leading indicators are strong, not using lagging indicators to decide whether to continue.

Monthly output check (inputs reviewed first): revenue or clients, physical performance metric, audience or reach metric, skill output metric. If your monthly output metrics show no movement, that's expected during the Evidence Gap, not a signal to stop. The compound is building. Keep building.

WHAT ONE WEEK OF TRACKING LOOKS LIKE

Abstract systems become real through examples. Here is one week of daily tracking for someone building a new skill, in this case, learning to code from nothing with the goal of launching a simple web application.

Day	Executed? (Y/N)	Time Invested	One Thing I Learned or Adjusted
Monday	Y	1.5 hours	Variables and loops take longer to internalize than expected; repetition, not reading, is how they click.
Tuesday	Y	30 minutes	Even on a brutal day, 30 minutes is infinitely more than zero; wrote one working function.
Wednesday	Y	2 hours	The error in yesterday's code was a missing closing bracket; pattern recognition is developing.
Thursday	Y	2 hours	Fixed the error; the function runs correctly; first working piece of the application exists.
Friday	N	0	Skipping happens; the rule is never skip twice.
Saturday	Y	1 hour	Getting back on track after one miss requires less energy than assumed.
Sunday	Y	2 hours	Weekly review completed.

WEEKLY SUMMARY:

6/7 days executed. 9 total hours. System working. Adjustment for next week: schedule Tuesday session before 7am to protect Tier 1 even on full days. Evidence collected: first working function built and de-

bugged, demonstrating that pattern recognition is developing faster than week one.

Notice what that weekly summary does not contain: whether anyone hired them, whether the application has users, or whether anyone cares. Those are output metrics. They aren't available yet, and they aren't the point of this week's tracking. The point is to confirm that inputs are happening and that small adjustments are being made.

THE EVIDENCE COLLECTION SYSTEM

One of the primary reasons people interpret the Evidence Gap as failure is that they are only looking for one type of evidence: the big outcome. Revenue. Audience size. Published work. Weight lost. Muscle built. As long as that evidence is absent, they conclude that what they are doing isn't working, and they change it or they quit.

Underground growth produces five types of evidence, and four of them are available long before the big outcome arrives. The Evidence Collection System trains you to see all five every week. After twelve weeks, you will have collected sixty or more data points proving that the work is happening and compounding, even while the main outcome metric sits at zero.

NOTE: *The Diagnostic Framework in Chapter 8 helps you identify whether your process is working. The Evidence Collection System below helps you see and document the proof that it is, even before the main outcome arrives. They serve different purposes and complement each other.*

Evidence Type 1: Capability Evidence

What can you do now that you couldn't do thirty days ago? What takes thirty minutes that previously took two hours? What problems can you solve that you could not solve six weeks ago?

A person learning to code at month two produces cleaner functions than at month one. A parent working on a difficult relationship at month four handles conversations that would have paralyzed them at month one. A new runner at month three recovers faster than at month one. Track this specifically. "I can now debug a Python error in fifteen minutes that used to take me two hours" is capability evidence. It's real, it's verifiable, and it's proof that your work is compounding.

Evidence Type 2: Response Evidence

How are people responding to your work, your presence, or your efforts differently than they were thirty days ago? Are conversations going longer? Are people asking follow-up questions instead of politely changing the subject? Are the responses you receive becoming more specific and engaged rather than generic?

The colleague who stops to ask what you have been working on rather than making polite conversation is a response to evidence. The person who remembered something you said last month and brought it up unprompted is a response to evidence. The coach or instructor who pushes you harder because they can see you are ready is a response to evidence. None of it is the big outcome. All of it is evidence of underground movement.

Evidence Type 3: System Evidence

Are your systems running more smoothly than they were thirty days ago? Are you executing with less friction? Are decisions that required deliberate thought becoming automatic?

System evidence proves that the behavioral infrastructure you built in Chapters 4 through 7 is maturing. When your discipline system requires less willpower to maintain, that is evidence. When your decision-making process produces faster, more confident calls than it did at month one, that is evidence. When your adjustment cycle is tighter and more accurate, that is evidence. The systems are becoming load-bearing, which is exactly what they need to be before the big outcome can stand on them.

Evidence Type 4: Learning Evidence

What do you know now that you did not know thirty days ago? What mistakes have you stopped making? What patterns have you recognized?

In 1953, the Rocket Chemical Company in San Diego set out to create a water-displacement formula to protect metal parts from rust and corrosion. They failed thirty-nine times before the fortieth attempt worked. They called the product WD-40, Water Displacement, 40th formula, a name the company kept simply because it was an accurate record of the process. Each of the thirty-nine failed formulas was learning evidence: what did not work, which paths were closed, which variables mattered. Without the thirty-nine failures, the fortieth formula would not have existed.

That learning did not belong to any single attempt. It belonged to the chemists, and it was compounded in them, available for every subsequent try. If the fortieth formula had also failed, those chemists would still have been among the most knowledgeable people on earth about water-displacement chemistry.

Track your learning evidence weekly. What did this week teach you that you will carry into next week? What you can't do yet is output evidence. What you now know is learning evidence, and it's available to you right now.

Evidence Type 5: Progress Evidence

Where are you in the process relative to thirty days ago? Not in terms of outcome, in terms of position within the system you are building.

If you wrote three thousand words this week. Maybe you don't have a published book yet, but three thousand more words of it exist than did last Monday. You held five difficult conversations with your child. No breakthrough yet, but five more attempts at connection occurred than the week before. You ran three training sessions. No visible physical change yet, but three more sessions of neurological adaptation have happened. Progress evidence is cumulative and directional. It tells you that you are moving through the Evidence Gap toward the outcome, even when the outcome is not in sight.

THE WEEKLY EVIDENCE REVIEW

Every Sunday evening, before your weekly tracking review, answer these five questions. One answer per question.

Capability: What can I do now that I could not do 30 days ago?:

____

Response: How did people respond to my work or efforts differently this week than last month?:

____

System: What ran more smoothly this week than it did 30 days ago?:

____

Learning: What did I learn this week that changes how I will work next week?:

____

Progress: Where am I now compared to 30 days ago in absolute terms?: _______________________________________

After twelve weeks of this review, you will have sixty answers across five categories. Read them in sequence from week one to week twelve. You will see a pattern that was invisible week by week. The capability was building. The responses were shifting. The systems were hardening. The learning was compounding. The position was advancing. The underground work was always ongoing. You just could not see the pattern until you had enough data points to connect.

BUILDING RESILIENCE THROUGH THE GAP

When you're in the gap, nothing about it feels comfortable or easy, and it can take a toll on you. Here are three strategies for helping you survive the gap operationally, when understanding why it exists doesn't make living through it feel any better.

Strategy 1: Create Checkpoints, Not Endpoints

Most people set a single endpoint: the goal achieved. The book was published. The business is profitable. The weight reached. When that endpoint doesn't arrive on schedule, which it won't, because the schedule was built on a planning fallacy, there is nothing to show for your effort, and the default response is to interpret the delay as failure.

Replace the single endpoint with multiple checkpoints that measure process milestones rather than outcome milestones. For a person rebuilding their fitness: tracking system installed and running by the end of month one; eighty percent or higher execution rate established by month two; at least one capability improvement documented per week; evidence review showing compound across all five categories before the end of month six.

The specific checkpoints depend on your domain. The principle is universal: build process milestones you can hit or miss, regardless of whether the outcome has arrived yet. Hit most of them, and the system is working. The outcome is coming. You are not failing. You are on schedule.

Strategy 2: Document Small Wins and Tell Someone

Your Evidence Collection System handles the documentation. The strategy here goes one step further: share the wins with someone who understands what they mean.

A capability win that stays in your journal can be dismissed by the internal voice that says the progress isn't real. A capability win that you tell your accountability partner, who confirms they noticed the same thing, becomes harder to dismiss. Small wins lose power in isolation. They gain power in connection. Document them. Then tell someone.

Strategy 3: Build Your Support Structure

The cultural narrative around the Evidence Gap is almost always solo: the lone inventor in the garage, the writer in the cabin, the athlete training before dawn in an empty gym. That narrative is accurate as a description and dangerous as a prescription. Surviving the Evidence Gap alone is significantly harder than surviving it with support.

Build three types of support before you need them, not after they become urgent.

An accountability partner: one person who knows your goal, knows your weekly commitment, and checks in with you. Not to judge your outcome metrics, but to ask whether you executed your inputs this week. All you need is a few minutes of weekly contact. Accountability transforms intention into action more reliably than motivation does.

A community of people in the same phase: people who are also in the Evidence Gap of a similar pursuit. The value here is normalization. Hearing someone else describe Stage 3 and recognizing your own experience in it prevents the misdiagnosis of the grind as personal failure.

A mentor or coach who has survived the gap: someone who has already been through the Evidence Gap in your domain and came out the other side. Not to tell you what to do, just to show you, by their existence, that Stage 4 arrives. A mentor who survived Stage 3 is proof that Stage 4 is real, and you can get through it.

RECOGNIZING BREAKTHROUGH INDICATORS

One of the most common failures inside the Evidence Gap is quitting right before the breakthrough happens. Not because people are weak, tons of tough people have given up too soon, and you probably know someone. It's because the breakthrough doesn't announce itself. Stage 4 doesn't begin with a door opening. It begins with signals so subtle that most people either miss them or dismiss them as mere coincidence.

Here are six signals that the compounding is beginning to surface. If you see two or more in the same week, accelerate your inputs. This isn't the time to coast. This is the time to double down.

Signal 1: The Second Conversation

Someone follows up with you without being prompted. They reached out before you did. They remembered something you said or did and came back to it. This isn't small talk. It means they thought about between the time they left and now. Unprompted follow-up is one of the clearest signals that something you're doing has crossed a visibility threshold.

Signal 2: The Unsolicited Question

Someone asks what you are doing, what system you are using, or how you accomplished something, without you mentioning it first. They noticed a change that you did not announce. Changes you did not announce are changes that became visible on their own. That means the compound crossed a threshold. Something underground has surfaced.

Signal 3: The Pattern Shift

You realize you are solving problems faster than you were two months ago. Decisions that required research now feel intuitive. Skills that required concentration now feel natural. The pattern recognition that was building underground has surfaced as actual competence. You're not performing capability. You have it.

Signal 4: The Confidence Increase

This isn't performed confidence. It's not bravado. Actual procedural confidence is: you know what to do next without having to stop and think about it. The gap between intention and execution has narrowed. This is a leading indicator of Stage 4. The system has become internal. You're no longer running the system, the system is running you.

Signal 5: The Small Cluster

Three or more small positive signals in the same week. Not one standout moment. A cluster of quiet confirmations: a conversation that went unusually well, a piece of work that landed differently than expected, and feedback that was qualitatively different from what you had been receiving. No single item is dramatic. The cluster is. Clusters are how Stage 4 announces itself, quietly, in groups, before the obvious breakthrough arrives.

Signal 6: The Response Upgrade

The quality of the responses you receive changes. Instead of indifference or flat dismissal, you start receiving more specific, more engaged reactions, whether that's in your work, your relationships, your training, your creative output, or any other domain you're building in. The engagement isn't necessarily positive, but it's specific. Specificity means you're being taken seriously. You have crossed a credibility threshold. The compounding has done enough work that the nature of the conversation has changed as a result of it.

THE INVISIBLE WORK IS NEVER WASTED

Here is the concern that lives underneath the Evidence Gap and rarely gets named directly: what if I do all of this and the goal never materializes? What if I execute for eighteen months and the business fails, the project goes unpublished, and the outcome never comes? Did I waste eighteen months? No. And here's why.

The same compounding that turned thirty-nine failed formulas into WD-40 applies to every input you make. But consider what those thirty-nine failures built: a depth of knowledge about water displacement, material science, manufacturing constraints, and iterative problem-solving that belonged to the chemists, not to any single formula. If the fortieth formula had also failed, they would still have been among the most knowledgeable people on earth in their domain. The knowledge was not conditional on the outcome.

The inputs build capability that belongs to you regardless of whether any specific goal materializes. The writing sessions that produce no published book produce a writer. The training sessions that produce no visible physique produce a trained body. The difficult conversations that produce no immediate resolution build a person who can hold difficulty without breaking. The sales calls that produce no clients produce a salesperson who knows exactly how to have the next conversation differently.

The work is building you. You carry that compound forward into every subsequent attempt. No input is ever truly wasted, because every input that did not produce the intended outcome produced something else: a more capable, more knowledgeable, more resilient person who is better positioned for the next attempt than they were for the last one.

The compound does not live in the outcome. It lives in you. Every input builds you, regardless of what the outcome does.

THE 90-DAY TRUST CHALLENGE

This is the complete operational commitment for executing through the Evidence Gap. It incorporates the Process Metrics System, the Evidence Collection System, and all three resilience strategies into one signed commitment.

> *I commit to executing my system for 90 days, targeting full execution, your emergency minimum, or your contingency protocol (from Chapter 6) every day, with a target execution rate of 95 percent or higher, never missing two consecutive days.*

> *I commit to tracking daily inputs (three data points: executed Y/ N, hours invested, one lesson learned), weekly inputs (five data points Sunday: days executed, total hours, system working Y/N, one adjustment, one piece of evidence), and monthly inputs with a single output check only after the input review is complete.*

I commit to not using output metrics to decide whether to continue before Day 91.

I commit to building my support structure before I need it: an accountability partner, a community, and a mentor or coach.

I commit to applying my realistic timeline, my original estimate extended significantly for the planning fallacy, and holding to it.

I commit to recognizing the six breakthrough signals and accelerating inputs when I see two or more in the same week.

My domain:

____

My original timeline estimate: _______________

My realistic timeline (extended): _______________

My current stage (1 through 5, from Chapter 8):

____

My accountability partner:

____

My community:

____

My mentor or coach:

____

Signed: ___________________________________

Date: _______________________________

Remember, knowing the Evidence Gap is structurally normal doesn't make it emotionally bearable. Tracking inputs instead of outputs, collecting evidence weekly, creating checkpoints instead of endpoints, building a support structure around you, and learning to read breakthrough signals make it survivable.

The work is happening, and the evidence is there; you just have to know where to find it.

CHAPTER 9 SUMMARY

- The core shift is measuring inputs you control rather than outputs you don't. Output metrics during the Evidence Gap produce despair because the outputs are underground by definition. The Control Principle draws the line: you control whether you execute today. You do not control when the audience finds you, when the business turns, or when the skill clicks.

- The Process Metrics System makes this concrete across three levels: three data points daily (executed Y/N, hours invested, one lesson learned), five data points every Sunday (days executed, total hours, system working Y/N, one adjustment, one evidence item), and one monthly review with a single output check only after inputs are confirmed. Never use output metrics to decide whether to continue before Day 91.

- The Evidence Collection System trains you to see five types of underground progress every week: capability evidence (what you can do now that you couldn't thirty days ago), response evidence (how people respond differently than last month), system evidence (what runs with less friction than before), learning evidence (what this week taught you, the same compounding that turned 39 failed formulas into WD-40), and progress evidence (where you are in the process relative to thirty days ago). After twelve weeks of Weekly Evidence Reviews, you will have sixty or more data points proving the work is compounding even while the main metric sits at zero.

- The invisible work is never wasted. Every input that did not produce the intended outcome produced something else: a more capable, more resilient person better positioned for the next attempt. The compound does not live in the outcome. It lives in you.

- Three resilience strategies sustain you through Stage 3: create process-milestone checkpoints instead of a single outcome endpoint, document small wins and tell someone so they cannot be privately dismissed, and build your support structure, an accountability partner, a community, and a mentor, before you need it. When two or more of the six breakthrough signals appear in the same week, accelerate inputs. That is Stage 4 announcing itself quietly before the obvious breakthrough arrives.

WHAT'S NEXT

Chapters 1 through 9 have given you the complete execution system: action creates clarity, identity drives results, the Discipline Operating System and the emergency minimum framework (Chapter 6), faster decisions and decision velocity (Chapter 7), results lag and inputs compound, and tracking the underground work.

Chapter 10 integrates all of it. Not as a summary but as a compound: how the five principles interact and reinforce each other when they are running simultaneously, how each one compounds the others, and how to sustain the complete system across the full arc of any meaningful goal.

Start the 90-Day Trust Challenge today. Chapter 10 will land differently once you have real tracking data behind you than it will if you read it cold. Either way, keep moving.

SECTION 7
INTEGRATION

10. THE COMPLETE SYSTEM

"You do not need all five principles perfect. You need all five principles running. The integration is the point. The integration is the product."

Chapters 1 through 9 gave you the five principles: Action Creates Clarity. Identity Drives Results. Discipline Beats Motivation. Decide Fast, Adjust Faster. Trust the Invisible Work. You have read the stories, worked through the frameworks, and started applying each principle individually.

This is where some readers stop. They pick the one or two principles that resonate most strongly and apply those. The person who loves taking action ignores discipline systems. The person who loves systems never validates through action first. The person who builds identity never develops decision velocity. The person who develops velocity never learns to trust the gap.
That selective application feels efficient, but it's actually the reason most people's goal attempts eventually break down.

The five principles aren't five separate techniques; they are five components of a single integrated system. Applied together, with each one running simultaneously and reinforcing the others, they create something that none of them can produce alone: compound momentum that becomes self-sustaining. If you remove any one component, the system doesn't produce 80 percent of its potential. It degrades, sometimes catastrophically.

This chapter shows you how the integration works, how it breaks, and what to do when one principle gets hard while the others are running.

THE EXECUTION COMPOUND

Think of the five principles as interlocking gears. When all five are meshing, turning one gear causes all of them to turn, and the system generates momentum that no single gear could produce alone. Remove one gear, and the train does not slow down. The connection breaks. The system stops.

What this integrated system produces is what I call the Execution Compound: the accumulated momentum that builds when all five principles run simultaneously, each one driving the next, each turn of the system adding to every previous one. It is not five separate gears spinning independently alongside each other. It is five gears meshing together to drive something none of them could move alone.

Jeff Bezos applied similar logic at the corporate level when he sketched what he called the virtuous cycle on a napkin in 2001, during the dot-com collapse: lower prices attract more customers, more customers attract more sellers, more sellers expand selection, expanded selection lowers costs, lower costs enable lower prices, and around it goes. Amazon didn't turn its first annual profit until 2003, seven years after founding. The cycle was turning the entire time, but the big outcome wasn't visible yet.

The Execute First system applies the same integration logic at the individual level.

HOW THE PRINCIPLES REINFORCE EACH OTHER

Here is the integration in motion. Not sequentially, one principle after another, but simultaneously, all five running at the same time, each one accelerating the others.

Action Creates Clarity generates real-world data about what works. That data gives you specific evidence of who you are capable of being, which is the raw material that Identity Drives Results runs on. The clearer your identity becomes through accumulated action evidence, the more natural your daily consistency feels, which is the foundation that Discipline Beats Motivation requires. Strong discipline systems reduce the cost of each execution decision, which is what enables Decide Fast, Adjust Faster to operate at the velocity it needs. Rapid adjustment based on real feedback shortens your execution timeline precisely because you stop forcing what doesn't work, which is what Trust the Invisible Work requires to protect the compound during the gap between effort and evidence.

Then the cycle accelerates. Trusting in the invisible work allows you to take more action without panic or doubt. More action generates more clarity. More clarity deepens identity. Deeper identity strengthens discipline naturally. Stronger discipline enables faster decisions. Faster decisions create more action. And each cycle of the Execution Compound builds on every previous cycle.

Every principle feeds every other principle. Remove one, and the Execution Compound doesn't slow down. The whole system stops.

The interactions between principles aren't just circular though; each principle pair has a specific reinforcement mechanism.

Action (Principle 1) + Identity (Principle 2): Every time you take action and survive it, you collect evidence of capability. That evidence is the raw material of identity. Identity formed through action evidence is more durable than identity formed through affirmations or intentions, because it is backed by facts you lived through. The Identity Ledger from Chapter 5 is where that evidence accumulates. And the stronger that identity, the more naturally the next action follows.

Identity (Principle 2) + Discipline (Principle 3): When you have claimed a specific identity, executing your discipline system stops being an act of willpower and starts being an act of consistency with who you are. "I am someone who works out every day" doesn't require motivation. It only requires that you act like the person you already decided you are. Identity makes discipline automatic rather than effortful.

Discipline (Principle 3) + Decision Velocity (Principle 4): A consistent discipline system generates enough execution volume that you make decisions frequently. And frequency is what creates judgment. The person who has made 500 decisions in their domain over six months has faster and more accurate judgment than the person who has made five. Discipline creates the repetition that makes velocity safe.

Decision Velocity (Principle 4) + Trust (Principle 5): Rapid adjustment based on real feedback means you aren't forcing approaches that have stopped working. You adjust before you burn out. That adjustment capability is what makes long-term trust in invisible work emotionally sustainable. You are not asking yourself to persist blindly. You are persisting intelligently while adjusting course based on what you learn.

Trust (Principle 5) + Action (Principle 1): When you genuinely trust that the invisible work compounds, you take more action without requiring immediate proof that it is working. That bias toward action generates more clarity. The invisible work gives you the security to keep moving even when the feedback loop is slow. Trust in the process makes action sustainable across the full long-term arc.

THE INTEGRATION IN PRACTICE: YVON CHOUINARD

So far, every story in this book has illustrated one or two principles in depth. Jan Koum showed you how action creates clarity. Stephen King showed you how identity drives results. Jocko Willink showed you how discipline beats motivation. Paul MacCready showed you how decision velocity compounds. Antoni Gaudí showed you how invisible work builds structures that outlast the builder.

But none of those stories showed you all five principles running simultaneously in a single person's journey. That's what this section does. Because the integration isn't five principles applied in sequence. It's five principles operating at the same time, each one reinforcing the others, producing compound momentum that no single principle could generate alone.

In 1957, a teenage climber in Southern California had a problem. The European climbing pitons available at the time, metal spikes hammered into rock cracks to anchor a rope and protect the climber against a fall, were expensive, wasteful, and inadequate for the big granite walls of Yosemite, which is where Yvon Chouinard and his friends were beginning to climb.

Chouinard didn't sit around and study the problem. He didn't write a well thought out business plan. He didn't research metallurgy or take a blacksmithing course. He went to a junkyard, bought a used coal-fired forge and a 138-pound anvil for a few dollars, and taught himself to shape steel in his parents' backyard. Eventually, he started hammering out chrome-molybdenum pitons that were reusable, durable, and better than anything else on the market. He tested them on actual climbs. When they failed, he adjusted the design. When they bent, he changed the alloy. He sold them from the trunk of his car for $1.50 each while traveling to different climbing destinations.

By 1970, thirteen years after that junkyard purchase, Chouinard Equipment had become the largest supplier of climbing hardware in the United States. That operation would eventually evolve into Patagonia, a company now valued at over $3 billion and highly regarded all over the world. Here is what the integration of all five principles looked like across sixteen years of building.

Action Creates Clarity

Chouinard had no plan. He had a problem, and eventually he had a forge. Every piton he hammered taught him something about metallurgy, design tolerances, and what climbers actually needed in the field that no amount of research could have revealed. He iterated through dozens of designs before producing hardware that outperformed everything available. The action created his clarity.

Identity Drives Results

Chouinard identified as a climber who made gear. He never identified as a businessman who sold climbing equipment. This distinction drove every subsequent decision. His identity was rooted in the climbing community, in protecting the rock, in being a craftsman who happened to sell what he crafted. He referred to himself as a "dirtbag climber," and he meant it. He ate canned tuna and poached ground squirrel while he was on the road. He slept under rock faces and sold pitons between his climbs. When the business later confronted a values conflict, his identity resolved it instantly. A businessman would have optimized for revenue. A climber who made gear optimized for the rock instead.

Discipline Beats Motivation

For thirteen years, from 1957 to 1970, Chouinard made climbing hardware by hand. He forged pitons in the winter months when the rock faces were unclimbable and sold them in the summer while traveling to climbing destinations. He partnered with aeronautical engineer Tom Frost in 1965, and together they redesigned and improved every tool climbers used. This wasn't a motivated sprint. It was over a decade of consistent, seasonal, disciplined production:

forge in winter, sell in summer, test on climbs, adjust designs, repeat. The largest climbing hardware supplier in the United States was built on thirteen years of disciplined repetition, not a single breakthrough moment.

Decide Fast, Adjust Faster

In 1970, after climbing the Nose route on El Capitan, Chouinard and Frost saw that the repeated hammering and removal of their hard steel pitons was destroying the rock. The same cracks that had been pristine a few years earlier were now scarred, with flakes and slabs broken off.

Chouinard made a decision that would have paralyzed most business owners: he voluntarily killed 70 percent of his company's revenue by stopping the sale of his biggest seller.

He and Frost announced in the 1972 Chouinard Equipment catalog that the company would phase out piton production entirely and replace them with aluminum chocks, protection devices that could be wedged into cracks by hand without damaging the rock. The catalog opened with an editorial explaining the environmental damage pitons caused and included a 14-page essay by Sierra climber Doug Robinson on clean climbing technique. Chouinard didn't study the decision for years. He didn't commission market research. He saw the damage, identified the alternative, and committed to it. By Chapter 7's framework, this was a one-way door, consequential and largely irreversible. But when identity is clear enough, certain one-way door decisions carry no ambiguity. The framework tells you to slow down when you face genuine uncertainty. Chouinard had none. His identity removed the decision entirely. Within months of the catalog's mailing, the piton business had atrophied, and chocks were selling faster than Chouinard could manufacture them.

The decision was fast, values-driven, and irreversible. It was also correct. It transformed the entire climbing industry and established Chouinard's reputation as someone whose identity drove decisions that the market followed rather than dictated. Chouinard had thirteen years of immersion in his market. And he was applying deep, accumulated knowledge, which is exactly what behavioral revelation is designed to build.

Trust the Invisible Work

From the junkyard forge in 1957 to the founding of Patagonia in 1973, sixteen years elapsed. During those years, Chouinard was building expertise in materials science, manufacturing, supply chain logistics, community reputation, and product design. None of it was visible as a company to anyone outside of the climbing world. It was just a man in a backyard with an anvil, then a man selling gear from his car trunk, then a small operation in a tin shed in Ventura, California.

The invisible accumulation of those sixteen years became the foundation for Patagonia. The rugby shirts he bought on a trip to Scotland in 1970 and sold successfully to climbers became the seed of the clothing line. But the clothing line only worked because of the sixteen years of invisible work that preceded it: the community trust, the manufacturing knowledge, the identity as a craftsman, the reputation for putting values ahead of revenue. Remove any of those invisible inputs, and the clothing company would have had no foundation to stand on.

Action generated knowledge that built his identity as a craftsman whose values drove product decisions. Identity drove thirteen years of disciplined daily production. That consistency created the decision volume and pattern recognition that made the pivot feel obvious rather than terrifying. The decision to pivot was only possible because the identity was clear enough to override the financial logic. And the trust in invisible work sustained Chouinard through sixteen years of building something that did not look like a company until it became one that the entire world recognizes.

All five principles were running simultaneously. Not in sequence. Not one at a time. Each one reinforcing the others, each cycle of the compound building on every previous cycle. Remove any single principle, and the integration collapses at that point.

WHAT WOULD HAVE BROKEN THE COMPOUND

Action without identity: Without identity anchoring his actions to the climbing community, Chouinard's forging would have been just metalwork. Just products designed for revenue rather than for the rock. When the piton damage became visible, a profit-driven founder without a climber's identity likely would have ignored it or rationalized it. The pivot never happens, and the brand never forms. His identity is what made the pivot not just possible but obvious.

Identity without discipline: Chouinard could have called himself a climber-craftsman forever without producing hardware consistently for thirteen years. Identity without the daily work of forging, testing, and selling is aspiration, not execution. The reputation never builds. The community never trusts the gear.

Discipline without decision velocity: Grinding out pitons year after year past the point where the product was damaging the thing Chouinard loved most. High effort, wrong direction. The rock degrades. The community loses respect. The discipline becomes persistence applied to a broken, misdirected approach.

Decision velocity without trust: Pivoting from pitons to chocks and then checking revenue numbers weekly, panicking at the initial drop, second-guessing the catalog, reversing the decision three months later. The system never has time to build momentum. The market never follows.

Trust without action: Believing the invisible work would compound but not forging the pitons, not testing them on climbs, not selling them from the car, not publishing the catalog. Trust not backed by consistent inputs is not trust in the process. It's hope, and hope doesn't compound.

The Execution Compound requires all five gears. Not perfectly. Not without hard seasons. But consistently enough that the system never fully stops turning between cycles. Momentum that slows can be restored, but momentum that stops completely requires starting over. The Chouinard counterfactuals are specific to one story. The following four failure modes apply to every reader of this book.

An arch only stands when every stone is carrying a load. Remove one stone from the wrong position, and the arch does not carry 80 percent of the weight. It collapses completely. Gaudí understood this about stone. The Execution Compound works the same way. Every principle is a load-bearing stone. The integration is not an aspiration. It's the structural requirement.

FOUR WAYS THE INTEGRATION BREAKS DOWN

Understanding how the integration works is extremely valuable, but you also need to understand how it breaks, because the breaking patterns are predictable and diagnosable. And knowing them in advance means you can recognize them early and intervene before the system stops turning.

Failure Mode 1: Using One Principle Without the Others

The most common failure pattern is selective application. Someone reads this book, identifies Action Creates Clarity as their core challenge, and starts taking more action without installing any of the other four principles. They generate clarity through action. They get some momentum. Then, without an identity system, the action becomes inconsistent. Without discipline systems, bad weeks interrupt the compounding. Without decision velocity, they continue executing approaches that aren't working. Without trust in the invisible work, they quit at month four when the outcome hasn't appeared.

Action alone cannot sustain the Execution Compound. Neither can any other single principle. The system requires all five gears to turn simultaneously. With one gear turning and four disengaged, the gear train doesn't slow down. It doesn't move at all.

The fix isn't to abandon the strong principle. It is to identify which of the other four is weakest and install it next, while the strong one continues running.

Failure Mode 2: Scaling Before Validating

In 1998, Pets.com launched as an online retailer for pet supplies. Within two years, the company had raised over $300 million in funding, built warehouse infrastructure across the country, completed an IPO, and was running systems and operations at the scale of a mature company.

What they had not done was validate, at minimum viable scale, whether people would pay prices to have heavy pet supplies shipped to their homes at margins that made the business viable. They had built discipline systems at scale (Principle 3, Discipline Beats Motivation) and made confident scaling decisions (Principle 4, Decide Fast, Adjust Faster) before proving through real customer behavior at a small scale (Principle 1, Action Creates Clarity) that the fundamental premise was accurate.

This is an important distinction. Pets.com did take action. They launched a company, built infrastructure, and went public. But the action they took was not the Minimum Viable Action from Chapter 3. They skipped the smallest possible action that generates real data from the external world and went straight to scaled systems. The MVA for Pets.com would have been shipping pet food to a few hundred customers at sustainable prices and watching what happened. Instead, they shipped to many thousands of customers at subsidized prices and assumed the economics would improve at scale. They never validated the premise at a size where being wrong was cheap.

Pets.com completed its IPO on February 11, 2000. On November 7, 2000, 268 days later, it announced closure. The company had burned approximately $300 million in under two years. Not because the team lacked resources, systems, or decision-making capability. Because they applied Principles 3 and 4 at scale before Principle 1 had validated the premise at MVA scale.

The correct sequence always begins with Action Creates Clarity at a minimum viable scale, validating the core premise before building systems around it. Systems built before premise validation become very expensive to dismantle when the premise turns out to be wrong.

Failure Mode 3: Abandoning the Entire System When One Principle Gets Hard

This is the failure mode that destroys the most mature execution systems, because it happens to people who have already built real momentum. They have been executing for months. Multiple principles are running well. Then one principle hits a genuine difficulty: the Evidence Gap becomes brutal, a discipline streak breaks, or an identity belief gets shaken by a significant failure.

The natural response is to interpret the difficulty in that one principle as evidence that the entire system is not working. The discipline broke, so I must not be as disciplined as I thought. The Evidence Gap is going longer than expected, so the work must not be compounding. The identity belief wavered under pressure, so maybe I'm not who I claimed to be.

The system isn't broken. One gear in the system just encountered a hard period. The correct response is to diagnose which principle is struggling and address that specific principle while maintaining the others. Discipline broke? Drop to the Emergency Minimum from Chapter 6 and rebuild the streak. Trust is shaky? Return to the Evidence Collection System from Chapter 9 and collect data until the evidence outweighs the doubt. Identity wavered? Add one deliberate action that produces new capability evidence for your Identity Ledger.

Abandoning a mature Execution Compound because one gear got hard is like dismantling an arch because one stone became difficult to place. The momentum you built does not disappear instantly. But if you stop pushing entirely, it will stop eventually. Fix the weak gear while the rest keeps turning.

Failure Mode 4: Understanding Integration Without Implementing It Daily

This is the failure mode most likely to affect readers of this chapter specifically, because this chapter is the most conceptual chapter in the book. You can understand the Execution Compound perfectly and still not run it.

Understanding how the five principles interact doesn't make them interact. Daily implementation does. The Process Metrics System from Chapter 9 isn't optional infrastructure. It's the operational layer that makes the integration visible and measurable. Without daily input tracking, weekly evidence collection, and monthly output review, the integration exists only as a concept in your memory, not as a lived system producing compound momentum.

Chapter 11 provides the complete Execute First system: the daily checklist, weekly review, monthly audit, and diagnostic tools that make the Execution Compound operational rather than theoretical. Don't leave this chapter thinking that understanding the integration is the same as running it. Understanding is just the beginning. Implementation is where the compounding will come from.

THE INTEGRATION DIAGNOSTIC

Use this diagnostic monthly to identify which principle is your weakest link. Rate yourself honestly on each one from 1 to 5, where 1 means this principle is nearly absent from your current execution and 5 means it is fully operational and contributing to the Execution Compound.

Action Creates Clarity: Am I moving before I am ready and gathering real data through action, rather than planning until I feel confident?

Rating: ___ / 5

Identity Drives Results: Have I claimed a specific Bridge Identity, and am I collecting behavioral evidence in my Identity Ledger that confirms it through consistent execution?

Rating: ___ / 5

Discipline Beats Motivation: Is my discipline system running at a 95 percent or better execution rate, with a Full Version for normal days, an Emergency Minimum for low-motivation days, and a Contingency Protocol for when my standard environment is unavailable? Am I ever missing two consecutive days?

Rating: ___ / 5

Decide Fast, Adjust Faster: Am I making two-way door execution decisions within 48 hours at 70 percent confidence and adjusting based on real feedback rather than waiting for certainty?

Rating: ___ / 5

Trust the Invisible Work: Am I tracking inputs rather than obsessing over outputs, and maintaining the compound through the Evidence Gap without premature evaluation?

Rating: ___ / 5

Your lowest-rated principle is your weakest gear in the Execution Compound. It's also your highest-leverage point for improving the entire integration. The system only turns at the speed of its slowest gear.

WHAT TO DO WHEN THE COMPOUND PAUSES

The Execution Compound will pause at some point. It's inevitable. Business adversity hits. Personal circumstances intervene. A principle you thought was running well turns out to be running on stored momentum rather than active execution, and the compounding pauses.

When this happens, the instinct is to restart everything from scratch: re-read the whole book, redesign the system, give yourself a reset. Resist this. You don't restart a gear train by pulling it apart and starting over. You restart it by re-engaging the gear that stopped turning.

Use the Integration Diagnostic to identify which principle slowed. Then apply the specific repair for that principle.

Action slowed: Take one small action today, before any planning. The smallest possible action that is real and irreversible. Clarity follows.

Identity wavered: Name one thing you did in the last 30 days that the person you claimed to be would have done. One single piece of evidence. Add it to your Identity Ledger, then add to it tomorrow.

Discipline broke: Drop to the Emergency Minimum from Chapter 6. Not the Full Version. Not a major comeback effort. Just one day of executing the minimum. Then the next. Never miss two consecutive days.

Decision velocity dropped: Apply the Door Test from Chapter 7. Set a 48-hour decision deadline on the thing you've been avoiding deciding, then make the call with the information you have.

Trust collapsed: Open the Evidence Collection System from Chapter 9. Spend 20 minutes or so collecting evidence across all five categories. The evidence exists. You just stopped looking for it.

Focus on fixing the weak gear while the other four resume carrying their share of the load. The Execution Compound doesn't need a perfect cycle every time. It needs consistent cycles in the right direction, long enough for the momentum to become self-sustaining.

You don't need all five principles to be perfect. You need all five principles running. The integration is the point. The integration is the product.

CHAPTER 10 SUMMARY

- The five principles are not five separate techniques. They are five gears of the Execution Compound, and each one drives every other. Remove any single principle, and the system does not produce 80 percent of its potential. It stops.

- Each principle-pair has a specific reinforcement mechanism. Action builds capability evidence that Identity runs on. Identity makes Discipline automatic rather than effortful; you act like the person you decided to be, not the person you are trying to become. Discipline creates the decision volume that gives Decision Velocity the repetitions needed to produce accurate judgment. Rapid adjustment makes Trust in the invisible work emotionally sustainable; you are persisting intelligently, not blindly. Trust enables more action without requiring immediate proof, which generates more clarity and starts the cycle again.

- Yvon Chouinard's sixteen-year arc from a junkyard forge to Patagonia demonstrates the integration as lived experience: action-generated knowledge that built identity, identity drove thirteen years of disciplined hand manufacturing, discipline created the decision volume that made the piton-to-chocks pivot feel obvious rather than terrifying, and trust in invisible work sustained the compound through sixteen years before anything looked like a company.

- Removing any single principle would have stopped the system: action without identity produces behavior that cannot sustain a values test; identity without discipline is aspiration, not execution; discipline without decision velocity grinds in the wrong direction; decision velocity without trust panics at the first revenue dip and reverses course; trust without action is hope, and hope doesn't compound.

- Four failure modes break the integration: selective application (one principle without the others), scaling before validating (systems before the premise is proven at MVA scale, Pets.com burned $300 million in 268 days applying Principles 3 and 4 before Principle 1 had validated the premise), abandoning the entire system when one principle gets hard (the correct response is to repair the struggling gear while the others keep turning), and understanding the integration without implementing it daily.

- The Integration Diagnostic identifies your weakest gear monthly. Rate each principle 1 to 5. Your lowest score is your highest-leverage intervention point. When the compound pauses, do not restart from scratch. Apply the specific repair for the specific principle that slowed. The integration is the product.

WHAT'S NEXT

By now, integration lives in your daily decisions, weekly reviews, and monthly audits, not in conceptual understanding. Chapter 11: Your First 90 Days gives you the week-by-week roadmap that makes the system operational. A specific progressive build sequence across 90 days that tells you exactly what to do, and in what order, starting on Day 1.

You have the principles. You understand how they integrate. Chapter 11 gives you the daily infrastructure to run them. Don't skip it. The system turns in the implementation, not in the reading.

SECTION 8
YOUR ROADMAP

11. YOUR FIRST 90 DAYS

"The score takes care of itself."
— Bill Walsh

Most people who finish this book will close it, feel motivated for 48 hours, and return to their default patterns. This isn't a criticism. Unfortunately, it's a documented pattern in every domain of self-improvement. Motivation is real, but it's only temporary. The gap between reading about execution and actually executing is the same gap this entire book was written to close.

If you execute on it, this chapter closes that gap for you, with a specific week-by-week roadmap across 90 days that outlines exactly what to do on Monday morning, what to do in Week 5 when the doubt arrives, and what to do in Week 11 when impatience peaks.

By Day 84, you will have either a functioning integrated execution system or proof of which specific element broke and exactly how to repair it. Three months from now, you won't be in the same place. The question is only which direction you moved.

THE 90-DAY STRUCTURE

The roadmap is organized into three months, each building on the last. You don't implement all five principles simultaneously on Day 1. You layer them progressively, adding complexity only after the prior layer is operational.

Month 1 (Weeks 1 through 4): Foundation. Action Creates Clarity and Identity Drives Results. You audit where you stand, start moving, and connect daily action to the identity that gives it meaning.

Month 2 (Weeks 5 through 8): Systems and Velocity. Discipline Beats Motivation and Decide Fast, Adjust Faster. You stress-test the discipline framework from Chapter 6, build obstacle protocols, and begin practicing decision velocity through forced deadlines.

Month 3 (Weeks 9 through 12): Trust and Integration. Trust the Invisible Work and all five principles running simultaneously. You shift from output monitoring to input tracking, run the full Integration Diagnostic, and plan your next quarter.

Each month has four weeks. Each week has specific tasks, a success metric, and a pass or repeat criterion. The criterion is binary. You either completed the requirement or you repeat the week before advancing. There is no partial credit and no skipping ahead.

MONTH 1: FOUNDATION (WEEKS 1 THROUGH 4)

The goal of Month 1 is to establish daily movement and the identity that gives that movement meaning. By Day 28, you should have 20 or more days of execution documented and a Bridge Identity you can state from memory and actually believe.

Week 1: Audit, Commit, and Move

Days 1 through 7. Time required: 60 minutes on Day 1, 15 minutes per day after.

Day 1: Set Your Baseline and Commit.

Run the Integration Diagnostic from Chapter 10. If you completed the Integration Diagnostic in Chapter 10, retrieve those scores and use them as your Day 1 baseline here. If you have not yet run it, do so now before proceeding. Rate all five principles from 1 to 5. Write them down. These are your Day 1 scores. Without a baseline, the Day 84 comparison is meaningless.

Action Creates Clarity: ___/5

Identity Drives Results: ___/5

Discipline Beats Motivation: ___/5

Decide Fast, Adjust Faster: ___/5

Trust the Invisible Work: ___/5

Identify your accountability partner. Name them. Set a weekly check-in day and time. Text or call them today and tell them you are starting a 90-day execution build. Accountability installed on Day

1 runs the entire 90 days. Accountability installed on Day 84 runs nothing.

My accountability partner: ______________________________

Weekly check-in day and time: ______________________________

Confirm your MVA from Chapter 3. If you have been executing one since the 72-Hour Challenge, verify it still represents the smallest real action toward your current goal. If your goal has shifted, redefine it now. If your MVA is still accurate, write it here and move.

My MVA: ______________________________

Confirm your Bridge Identity from Chapter 5. If you defined one and it still fits, write it. If it needs adjustment based on what you have learned since Chapter 5, adjust it now.

My Bridge Identity: ______________________________

Days 2 through 7: Execute your MVA every day.

Six executions before Day 7. Document each one: Did I execute? Yes or No. Time invested. What I learned. Continue tracking Start Velocity from Chapter 4: note when you think about executing, note when you start, and track the gap.

PASS: MVA executed at least 5 of 6 days and documented by Day 7. Start Velocity tracked. Move to Week 2.

REPEAT: Fewer than 5 executions or not documented. Repeat before proceeding.

Week 2: Build Momentum and Start Weekly Review

Days 8 through 14. Time required: 15 minutes per day plus 10-minute review on Day 14.

Daily execution: Execute your MVA every day this week. Target 7 out of 7. Minimum acceptable: 5 out of 7. Before each execution, state your Bridge Identity aloud and connect it to the action. This is the identity-action connection from Chapter 5 reinforced through the Discipline Operating System in Chapter 6, not motivational theater. It is evidence collection.

Day 14: First Weekly Review. Install Chapter 9's weekly review and run it every week from here forward. 10 minutes. Record: total executions this week, average Start Velocity, which principle felt weakest this week, and one thing that surprised you about actually moving. This weekly cadence runs through Day 84.

PASS: 5 or more MVA executions documented. Weekly review completed. Move to Week 3.

REPEAT: Fewer than 5 executions or no weekly review. Repeat before proceeding.

Week 3: Test the Identity Connection

Days 15 through 21. Time required: 20 minutes per day.

You installed the Bridge Identity declaration in Chapter 6 and have been executing it for two weeks. This week's job is diagnostic: is the identity driving action automatically yet, or does it still require conscious effort?

Daily execution: 5 out of 7 minimum. After each execution, note whether the action felt like proof of the identity or like performance. The distinction will shift over time. Early in the process, performance is normal. By Week 3, you should notice at least some days where the action feels like evidence of who you are rather than something you are trying to become.

Day 21 diagnostic: Rate your belief in your Bridge Identity from 1 to 10 today versus Day 1. Write one specific action you took this week that the person you described would take.

PASS: 5 or more executions. Belief rating 5 or higher. Move to Week 4.

REPEAT: Fewer than 5 executions or belief rating below 5. Repeat before proceeding.

Week 4: Evidence Collection and Month 1 Review

Days 22 through 28. Time required: 20 minutes per day plus 1 hour on Day 28.

Start the Evidence Collection System from Chapter 9. If you started the Evidence Collection System in Chapter 9, continue it here; you may already have four weeks of entries. If you have not started it yet, begin this week. This is early and deliberate. The Doubt Phase arrives around Week 5. If you start collecting evidence now, you will have four weeks of entries to review when doubt hits instead of starting from zero when you need evidence most.

Each day, record at least one piece of evidence across any of the five categories from Chapter 9: capability evidence, response evidence, system evidence, learning evidence, or progress evidence. This takes two minutes, and it builds the trust foundation that Principle 5 requires.

Day 28 Month 1 Review:

Answer the following in writing before advancing to Month 2.

What clarity have I gained from 28 days of action that I did not have on Day 1?

How has my Bridge Identity changed or strengthened?

What is my average Start Velocity now versus Week 1?

Evidence entries collected: ___

Keep / Kill / Start: What do I keep, what do I eliminate, what do I add in Month 2?

PASS: 20 or more executions across 28 days. Month 1 review completed in writing. Evidence Collection started. Move to Month 2.

REPEAT: Fewer than 20 executions or review not completed. Repeat before proceeding.

MONTH 2: SYSTEMS AND VELOCITY (WEEKS 5 THROUGH 8)

The goal of Month 2 is to make execution automatic through systems rather than motivation, and to begin building decision velocity. By Day 56, your discipline framework should be running at 90% or better with documented evidence that it survived at least one difficult week. You should have made at least 20 decisions logged using the Door Test and 70% Rule from Chapter 7, roughly one per business day across four weeks.

Week 5: Stress-Test the Discipline System

Days 29 through 35. Time required: 30-minute review on Day 29, 20 minutes per day.

Day 29: Review your discipline framework from Chapter 6. You built this system in Chapter 6: the Full Version for normal days, the Emergency Minimum for days when motivation fails, and the Contingency Protocol for when your standard environment is unavailable. If you have not been running it consistently, this is the week to install it fully.

My Full Version: _______________________________

My Emergency Minimum: _______________________________

My Contingency Protocol: _______________________________

I   execute   the   Emergency   Minimum   when:

____

I   execute   the   Contingency   Protocol   when:

____

Days 30 through 35: Execute the Full Version or Emergency Minimum every day. The system has no zero days. Document which version you executed each day and why. The first time you execute the Emergency Minimum and maintain the streak rather than breaking it, that is the proof that the system works.

Decision velocity practice begins: For every execution-related decision you face this week, apply the Door Test from Chapter 7 before deliberating. Is it a one-way door or a two-way door? If two-way, decide within 48 hours at 70% confidence. Log one decision per day.

PASS: 7 out of 7 days executed. At least one Emergency Minimum day documented. 5 or more decisions logged. Move to Week 6.

REPEAT: Any zero-execution days. Repeat Week 5 until 7 out of 7 is achieved.

Week 6: Pre-Build Your Failure Protocols

Days 36 through 42. Time required: 30-minute protocol session on Day 36, 20 minutes per day.

Day 36: Write your specific obstacle protocols. Identify your three most predictable execution obstacles. Write a specific protocol for each one now, before they happen. A protocol is an if-then statement: If [specific obstacle], then I will [specific Emergency Minimum or Contingency Protocol action] at [time] in [location].

*Obstacle 1:*______________ *Protocol:*______________

*Obstacle 2:*______________ *Protocol:*______________

*Obstacle 3:*______________ *Protocol:*______________

Days 37 through 42: Continue executing Full Version or Emergency Minimum every day. Continue logging one decision per day using the 70% Rule. If any pre-built obstacle scenario occurs, execute the protocol exactly as written. Document whether it worked.

PASS: 7 out of 7 executions. 3 obstacle protocols written. Move to Week 7.

REPEAT: Any zero days or protocols not written. Repeat before proceeding.

Week 7: Force Decision Velocity

Days 43 through 49. Time required: 20 minutes per day plus decision log.

Day 43: Inventory your delayed decisions. Write down every meaningful decision related to your goal that has been sitting unresolved for more than 48 hours. Rank them by how long they have been avoided.

Days 44 through 49: Make at least one decision per day from your delayed list using a strict 24-hour deadline. The 70% Rule from Chapter 7 applies: if you have 70% of the information you wish you had, you have enough to decide. Document each decision: what it was, certainty level at decision time, what you decided, and what happened. Celebrate fast failures. A decision made at 70% certainty that produces a bad outcome within 48 hours is compressed learning. A decision avoided for two weeks that produces the same outcome is two weeks of wasted time.

PASS: 5 or more decisions made from the delayed list. All decided within 24 hours. Move to Week 8.

REPEAT: Fewer than 5 decisions or any decision delayed past 24 hours. Repeat before proceeding.

Week 8: Month 2 Review

Days 50 through 56. Time required: 20 minutes per day plus 90-minute review on Day 56.

Continue Full Version or Emergency Minimum daily. Continue decision logging.

Daily integration check begins: Starting this week and running through Day 84, ask yourself each evening: Did all five principles operate today? Not perfectly. Operationally. Mark yes or no for each. This keeps all five in view as you enter Month 3.

Day 56 Month 2 Review:

Days executed (Full Version): ___ of 28

Days executed (Emergency Minimum): ___ of 28

Zero days: ___ of 28

Decisions made using 70% Rule: ___

Obstacle protocols tested: ___ Did they work? ___

Evidence Collection entries to date: ___

How many days did you execute without motivation? What does that number prove about discipline versus motivation?

One system optimization based on 56 days of data:

____

PASS: 25 or more executions in Month 2. Review completed in writing. One optimization was identified. Move to Month 3.

REPEAT: Fewer than 25 executions or review incomplete. Repeat before proceeding.

MONTH 3: TRUST AND INTEGRATION (WEEKS 9 THROUGH 12)

The goal of Month 3 is to shift from output monitoring to input tracking, run the full integration with all five principles operating simultaneously, and plan your next quarter. By Day 84, you should be running Chapter 9's Process Metrics System daily, checking all five principles through the evening integration check, and evaluating your trajectory by inputs rather than outputs.

Week 9: Shift to Input Tracking

Days 57 through 63. Time required: 25 minutes per day.

Day 57: Timeline reality check.

What was your original timeline for seeing results from this 90-day effort? Write it down. Now apply the Invisible Multiplier Rule from Chapter 8: multiply by 2 to 2.5. That is your realistic timeline. You are not giving up. You are calibrating accurately.

My original timeline: _________________________________

My realistic timeline: _________________________________

Days 58 through 63: Stop monitoring outcomes daily. If you are checking outcome metrics (revenue, follower count, scale reading, responses, any output measure) more than once per week, you are monitoring too frequently for the compound timeline you are working within. Chapter 8 documented why daily outcome monitoring during the Evidence Gap produces misdiagnosis of progress as failure. Reduce to once per week maximum.

Continue running all systems: Full Version or Emergency Minimum daily, decision logging, daily integration check, weekly review. Add the Process Metrics System from Chapter 9 if you have not already installed it. You are now tracking inputs, not outputs.

PASS: Reduced to once-per-week outcome monitoring. Process Metrics are running daily. Move to Week 10.

REPEAT: Still checking outcomes daily. Repeat before proceeding.

Week 10: Build the Evidence Base for Trust

Days 64 through 70. Time required: 25 minutes per day.

By now, you should have five or more weeks of evidence entries from the Evidence Collection System. This week, the evidence base becomes your primary defense against the doubt that arrives in the final weeks.

Day 64: Evidence audit. Review every evidence entry from Week 4 forward. Count the entries by category. Identify which category has the most evidence and which has the least. For the weakest category, add three entries this week.

Continue all systems daily. Check the six breakthrough signals from Chapter 9. If two or more are present, the momentum is surfacing. Note them. If fewer than two are present, that is normal at this stage. Continue inputs.

PASS: Evidence audit completed. 3 new entries in the weakest category. All systems running. Move to Week 11.

REPEAT: Evidence audit not completed or systems not running. Repeat before proceeding.

Week 11: Run the Full Integration

Days 71 through 77. Time required: 25 minutes per day.

All five principles should now be running simultaneously. Action is generating clarity daily. The Bridge Identity is driving behavior rather than requiring conscious effort. The discipline framework is executing at 90% or better. Decision velocity has improved measurably from Week 5. Evidence is accumulating across all five categories.

This week, your only job is to run the system you built. No new frameworks. No adjustments. Execute the Full Version or Emergency Minimum daily, log decisions, run the evening integration check, conduct the weekly review, and track inputs through the Process Metrics System.

If any principle feels weak, apply the specific repair from Chapter 10's compound repair section. Don't redesign the entire system, just fix the weak element. The other four keep turning.

PASS: 7 out of 7 execution days. All five principles are operating on the evening integration check. Move to Week 12.

REPEAT: Any zero days or fewer than three principles operating consistently. Repeat before proceeding.

Week 12: The 90-Day Review

Days 78 through 84. Time required: 25 minutes per day plus a half-day review on Day 84.

Days 78 through 83: Continue all systems. No new frameworks. Run the system.

Day 84: The 90-Day Review.

Run the Integration Diagnostic from Chapter 10. Compare Day 84 ratings to your Day 1 baseline. The difference is quantifiable transformation.

Action Creates Clarity: Day 1:___ Day 84:___ Change:___

Identity Drives Results: Day 1:___ Day 84:___ Change:___

Discipline Beats Motivation: Day 1:___ Day 84:___ Change:___

Decide Fast, Adjust Faster: Day 1:___ Day 84:___ Change:___

Trust the Invisible Work: Day 1:___ Day 84:___ Change:___

Total executions across 84 days:___

Execution rate:___%

Decisions made using 70% Rule:___

Evidence entries collected:___

Timeline adjusted from___ to___

Plan your next 90 days. Q1 is complete. Q2 is about maintaining what you built and optimizing the weakest principle. Identify the principle with the lowest Day 84 rating. Write one specific action you will take in the first week of Q2 to strengthen it.

My Q2 focus principle:_______________________________

First action, Week 1 of Q2:_______________________________

PASS: Day 84 review completed. All five principles rated. Q2 focus identified. Q1 COMPLETE, SYSTEM ESTABLISHED.

THE FOUR PREDICTABLE OBSTACLES

These four obstacles will appear at approximately these points for most people. They aren't evidence of failure; they're stages of the system's timeline that almost everyone experiences. Knowing they are coming in advance changes your emotional relationship with them when they arrive.

Obstacle 1: The Week 3 Motivation Drop

What happens: The novelty of the new system wears off. Early execution stops feeling rewarding and starts feeling like a requirement.

Why: Dopamine normalization. The brain stops producing novelty rewards for behaviors it has categorized as routine.

The fix: Do not try to recreate the excitement. Execute the Emergency Minimum for three consecutive days. Do not assess the system during this phase. The goal is not to feel motivated. The goal is not to break the streak. See Chapter 6.

Obstacle 2: The Week 5 Doubt Phase

What happens: You have been executing for a month, and the results are not proportional to the effort. The rational part of your brain begins questioning whether the system is working.

Why: You are in the Evidence Gap from Chapter 8. Inputs are building, but the momentum isn't visible yet. Your evaluation interval is shorter than the compound timeline.

The fix: Extend your evaluation timeline using the Invisible Multiplier Rule. Open the Evidence Collection entries you started in Week 4. Read them. The evidence is already accumulating. The momentum is building. You are checking for results before they surface.

Obstacle 3: The Week 8 Plateau

What happens: The system is running. Discipline has automated. But progress feels flat. The gains of Month 1 are not repeating in Month 2.

Why: You are in the Grind Phase of the system's timeline from Chapter 8. The discipline is working, but the breakthrough has not arrived yet.

The fix: Do not redesign the system. Run the Month 2 Review. Identify one optimization and implement only that change. See Chapter 10 on Failure Mode 3: abandoning the system when one element gets hard.

Obstacle 4: The Week 11 Impatience Peak

What happens: You are 11 weeks in. The outcome is still not visible at the level you expected. The urge to quit or completely redesign the approach feels logical.

Why: You are near the end of the Grind Phase. The breakthrough is statistically close for people executing at your consistency level. The impatience peaks just before the momentum becomes visible, which is why most people quit at exactly this point.

The fix: Open your Evidence Collection entries. Read from Week 11 backward. Count the number of days you executed. Calculate your execution percentage. Check the six breakthrough signals from Chapter 9. The inputs are compounding. You are not failing. You are at the hardest point of the invisible phase. The people who persist through this point are the ones this book was written for.

WHAT IF I FALL BEHIND?

The 90-day plan assumes consistent execution, but life is not consistent. The Emergency Minimum from Chapter 6 exists specifically to ensure you never have a zero day. But if you are reading this section, and something interrupted your system, that's what this section is for.

If you miss 1 to 3 days: Do not restart from Day 1. Resume where you left off. Execute the Emergency Minimum for three consecutive days to rebuild momentum. Then continue the plan from your current week.

If you miss 1 or more full weeks: Diagnose first. Ask yourself honestly: did life interrupt (temporary), or did I quit (pattern)? If temporary, resume at the current week and extend your total timeline by the days missed. If pattern, return to Week 1 and rebuild the foundation.

If you complete Month 1 but skip Month 2: Do not advance to Month 3. Return to Week 5 and complete Month 2 before proceeding. Month 3 trust and integration require Month 2 discipline systems to be operational.

The principle: Progress is not linear. Falling behind does not mean starting over. The Execution Compound you built doesn't stop turning in a week. Resume, persist, and keep the system moving.

YOUR 90-DAY COMMITMENT

If you set up your accountability partner on Day 1 as instructed, this commitment makes that partnership concrete. If you skipped that step, go back and do it now. This commitment is a contract between you and the system you are building.

I understand that motivation will drop around Week 3 and that this is normal, not evidence of failure. I understand that results will lag behind inputs for months and that this is how the system works. I understand that I will face predictable obstacles at approximately Weeks 3, 5, 8, and 11, and that persisting through each one is the work.

I commit to executing my Full Version or Emergency Minimum every day for 84 days starting on the date below. I commit to completing each weekly review before advancing. I commit to diagnosing breaks using the Integration Diagnostic from Chapter 10 rather than abandoning the system.

Start date: _______________________

Day 84 date: _______________________

If I break this commitment before Day 84, I will:

____

The most effective commitment devices include a pre-specified consequence for breaking them, something specific and personally uncomfortable enough that avoiding it becomes easier than breaking the commitment. Research on commitment devices, a concept developed by behavioral economists including Dan Ariely and Klaus Wertenbroch at INSEAD, shows that pre-committing a specific, personally uncomfortable consequence for breaking a commitment significantly increases follow-through. The consequence does not need to be severe. It needs to be specific, real, and uncomfortable enough that not breaking the commitment is easier than paying the price.

Examples: donate $500 to a cause I do not support, publicly announce that I quit, write a detailed letter to my accountability partner explaining why I stopped, call one person I respect and tell them I did not follow through.

Signature: ___________________________

Date: _______________

Signing this is the first act of someone who runs the system rather than intends to run it. The gap between signing and not signing is exactly the gap this entire book is about.

WHAT HAPPENS AFTER DAY 84

Day 84 is the end of construction, not the end of execution. You have spent 12 weeks building a system. What comes next is running it. Continue the weekly review cadence. Run the Integration Diagnostic from Chapter 10 monthly. Address the weakest principle each quarter. The five principles stop being techniques and start being how you operate. That is the only finish line that matters.

CHAPTER 11 SUMMARY

- The 90-day roadmap closes the implementation gap by replacing motivation with a structured progressive build sequence.

Each week has specific tasks, a success metric, and a binary pass/repeat criterion. There is no partial credit and no skipping ahead.

- Four predictable obstacles arrive on schedule. The Week 3 Motivation Drop is dopamine normalization, execute the Emergency Minimum for three days without assessing. The Week 5 Doubt Phase is the Evidence Gap, extend your timeline and open your evidence entries. The Week 8 Plateau is the Grind, one optimization only, keep running. The Week 11 Impatience Peak is the most dangerous because it arrives just before the momentum becomes visible, review your entries, calculate your execution rate, check the breakthrough signals. The people who persist through this point are the ones this book was written for.

- If you fall behind: missing 1-3 days, resume and execute the Emergency Minimum for three consecutive days. Missing a full week, diagnose honestly, temporary interruption, or quit pattern? Temporary: resume and extend the timeline. Pattern: return to Week 1. If you complete Month 1 but skip Month 2, do not advance to Month 3.

- The commitment requires a named accountability partner, a pre-specified consequence for breaking it, and a signature. Research on commitment devices confirms that pre-committing a specific, uncomfortable consequence for breaking the commitment significantly increases follow-through. Day 84 is the end of construction, not the end of execution. The five principles stop being techniques and start being how you operate.

CONCLUSION

There is a story from ancient Greece about a philosopher named Zeno who constructed what he believed was perfect logical proof that motion was impossible. His argument was: to travel from any point A to any point B, you must first travel half the distance. Then half of what remains. Then half of that. Since this process of halving can continue infinitely, you can never actually arrive. Motion, Zeno concluded, was an illusion.

When the philosopher Diogenes heard this argument, he didn't attempt to refute it. He didn't gather evidence, construct a counterargument, or wait until he understood the mathematical solution. He stood up and walked across the room. The Latin phrase *"Solvitur ambulando,"* which means *"It is solved by walking,"* is attributed to Diogenes as a result of his argument to Zeno.

Those two words, *solvitur ambulando*, embody the title of this book and its message: Execute First. The Clarity Inversion you learned about, that the clarity you are waiting for only exists on the other side of the action you are avoiding, is solvitur ambulando. The Bridge Identity, that you become the person before the outcomes arrive, through daily behavior rather than external validation, is solvitur ambulando. The discipline system, the decision velocity, the

Evidence Gap, the tracking systems, every principle in this book is a different expression of the same ancient answer.

The problem is not solved by understanding it better. It's not solved by waiting for conditions to improve, for confidence to arrive, or for the right moment to reveal itself. It's solved by walking. By starting before you can see where you're going. By moving through the uncertainty rather than around it. Understanding doesn't move you forward. Execution does. That's been true since 300 BCE, and it's still true right now, at this moment, with this book in your hands.

Jan Koum walked. David Goggins walked. Stephen King walked, 2,000 words a day in a laundry room, one day at a time, long before a publisher said yes. Yvon Chouinard walked, sixteen years of forging pitons and selling gear from the trunk of his car before anyone would have called it a company.

None of them solved the problem by thinking about it.

The five principles in this book are not five separate ideas; they are five ways of saying the same thing: the path reveals itself to those who walk it. Action creates clarity. Identity forms through behavior. Discipline is what keeps you walking when motivation stops. Velocity is how fast you take each step. Trust is what lets you keep walking when you can't see what's ahead.

The Execution Compound doesn't require a perfect turn. It merely requires a consistent one, in the same direction, long enough for the momentum to become self-sustaining. What you build from here won't be the result of any single decision, any single day, or any single chapter you read. It will be the accumulated result of walking, of taking the next step when you didn't know which one was supposed to come after it.

The gap between where you are and where you want to be can always be divided in half again, and half again, until it looks infinite and the waiting seems rational.

But the answer hasn't changed in 2,400 years.

Stand up and walk across the room. *Solvitur ambulando.*

Execute first.

Execute First

NOTES

In this section you will find the references, sources and citations that I've used in the writing of this book. I have done everything I can to accurately cite information but if there is something that I missed or that is inaccurate, please reach out to me and I will update and revise as needed. You can find the most current and updated notes and citations at www.executefirstbook.com/notes.

CHAPTER 1 CITATIONS

1 Jan Koum background and WhatsApp origin: Olson, P. (2014, February 19). Billionaire's Row: The Race to Acquire WhatsApp. Forbes. / Wikipedia: WhatsApp, History and Background sections. / WhatsApp Inc. incorporation: Delaware Secretary of State records, February 24, 2009.

2 Color Labs funding and team details: TechCrunch (2011, March 23). Color Raises $41 Million In Funding For Its iPhone App. / Wikipedia: Color (company). / Bilton, N. (2011, March 25). Color Labs' App Launches to Confusion. The New York Times.

3 Color Labs App Store rating and initial user reception: Bilton, N. (2011, March 25). Color Labs' App Launches to Confusion. The New York Times.

4 Iyengar, S. S. & Lepper, M. R. (2000). When Choice Is Demotivating: Can One Desire Too Much of a Good Thing? Journal of Personality and Social Psychology, 79(6), 995–1006. Three experimental studies conducted in both field and laboratory settings. Study 1 (field): tasting booth at Draeger's Grocery, Menlo Park, California. Shoppers offered 6 jam varieties purchased at approximately ten times the rate of those offered 24 varieties. Studies 2 and 3 (laboratory): participants choosing from limited sets of chocolate options and essay topics reported greater satisfaction and produced better work than those given extensive sets. Conclusion: past a certain threshold, additional choice does not improve decisions — it prevents them.

CHAPTER 2 CITATIONS

1 Gene Hackman — lowest score at Pasadena Playhouse: Playbill (2025, February 27). Oscar Winning Actor Gene Hackman Dies at 95. playbill.com. / Wikipedia: Gene Hackman. / Deseret News (1988, August 18). Gene Hackman: Least Likely to Succeed?

2 Hackman and Hoffman "Least Likely to Succeed" designation and Hackman's move to New York: Playbill (2025, February 27). / NBC Los Angeles (2025, February). The Southern California Connection: Gene Hackman Took Acting Leap at Pasadena Playhouse. Note: A quote attributed to Hackman in earlier drafts has been removed. The original datable interview could not be confirmed. The

characterization appears as reported behavior rather than direct quotation.

3 Dustin Hoffman on Hackman's naturalistic acting style: Multiple biographical sources confirm that Hoffman attributed Hackman's unconventional approach to a naturalism misunderstood by conventional theatrical instructors. The Actors Pad (2016, May). Roommates Hackman and Hoffman Labelled "Least Likely to Succeed." theactorspad.com.

4 Hackman's career: Academy Award wins, career breakthrough, and biographical timeline: Wikipedia: Gene Hackman. / Playbill (2025, February 27).

5 Education system and risk-aversion conditioning: Robinson, K. (2006). Do Schools Kill Creativity? TED Talk. / Duckworth, A. (2016). Grit: The Power of Passion and Perseverance. New York: Scribner.

6 Fast decision-making and firm performance: Eisenhardt, K. M. (1989). Making Fast Strategic Decisions in High-Velocity Environments. Academy of Management Journal, 32(3), 543–576.

7 Social comparison and validation dependency: Vogel, E. A., Rose, J. P., Roberts, L. R., & Eckles, K. (2014). Social Comparison, Social Media, and Self-Evaluation. Psychology of Popular Media Culture, 3(4), 206–222. / Buunk, A. P. & Gibbons, F. X. (2007). Social Comparison: The End of a Theory and the Emergence of a Field. Organizational Behavior and Human Decision Processes, 102(1), 3–21.

8 Process orientation and persistence: Elliot, A. J. & Harackiewicz, J. M. (1996). Approach and Avoidance Achievement Goals and In-

trinsic Motivation. Journal of Personality and Social Psychology, 70(3), 461–475. / Duckworth, A. (2016). Grit. New York: Scribner.

9 Bandura, A. (1977). Self-Efficacy: Toward a Unifying Theory of Behavioral Change. Psychological Review, 84(2), 191–215. / Bandura, A. (1997). Self-Efficacy: The Exercise of Control. New York: W. H. Freeman and Company.

10 Gollwitzer, P. M. (1999). Implementation intentions: Strong effects of simple plans. American Psychologist, 54(7), 493–503. Foundational paper establishing implementation intention theory. Pre-specifying a situational trigger and behavioral response in if-then form delegates control of goal-directed behavior to environmental cues, removing the need for in-the-moment deliberation. The approach roughly doubles follow-through compared to goal intentions alone.

11 Gollwitzer, P. M. & Sheeran, P. (2006). Implementation intentions and goal achievement: A meta-analysis of effects and processes. Advances in Experimental Social Psychology, 38, 69–119. Meta-analysis of 94 independent studies involving more than 8,000 participants. Found a medium-to-large effect size (d = 0.65) for implementation intentions on goal attainment, above and beyond the effect of motivation alone.

12 Cialdini, R. B. (1984). Influence: The Psychology of Persuasion. New York: William Morrow and Company. Chapter 3 establishes the commitment and consistency principle: written, voluntary commitments create internal pressure to behave consistently because inconsistency threatens self-image.

Epigraph note: The William James quote ("Act as if what you do makes a difference. It does.") is confirmed in multiple James biographies and scholarly sources as representative of his documented views on will and habit.

CHAPTER 3 CITATIONS

1 LinkedIn launch date, co-founders, and early platform features: Wikipedia: LinkedIn. / LinkedIn About page: about.linkedin.com. / Reid Hoffman Wikipedia biography. Co-founders confirmed: Allen Blue, Konstantin Guericke, Eric Ly, and Jean-Luc Vaillant. Launch date: May 5, 2003.

2 LinkedIn first-month membership of approximately 4,500: Office Timeline (officetimeline.com). LinkedIn History and Development. Note: This figure represents end-of-first-month total, confirmed via multiple secondary sources.

3 LinkedIn growth milestones and Hoffman's iterative development methodology: Hoffman, R. & Casnocha, B. (2012). The Start-Up of You. New York: Crown Business. / Wikipedia: LinkedIn (1 million users August 2004; profitability March 2006).

4 Microsoft acquisition of LinkedIn for $26.2 billion, June 13, 2016: Wikipedia: LinkedIn. / Reid Hoffman Wikipedia biography.

5 Predictive processing and the unreliability of novel-outcome prediction: Clark, A. (2016). Surfing Uncertainty: Prediction, Action, and the Embodied Mind. Oxford University Press. / Friston, K. (2010). The Free-Energy Principle: A Unified Brain Theory? Nature Reviews Neuroscience, 11(2), 127–138.

6 Iteration velocity and innovation learning: Thomke, S. (2003). Experimentation Matters: Unlocking the Potential of New Technologies for Innovation. Harvard Business Press. / Thomke, S. & Fujimoto, T. (2000). The Effect of "Front-Loading" Problem-Solving on Product Development Performance. Journal of Product Innovation Management, 17(2), 128–142.

7 Intention-behavior gap and self-reinforcing delay: Sheeran, P. (2002). Intention-Behavior Relations: A Conceptual and Empirical Review. European Review of Social Psychology, 12(1), 1–36. / Steel, P. (2007). The Nature of Procrastination: A Meta-Analytic and Theoretical Review of Quintessential Self-Regulatory Failure. Psychological Bulletin, 133(1), 65–94.

Epigraph note: The E. M. Forster quote ("How do I know what I think until I see what I say?") is sourced from Forster, E. M. (1927). Aspects of the Novel. London: Edward Arnold.

CHAPTER 4 CITATIONS

1 David Goggins — background, weight, exterminator employment, and enlistment story: Goggins, D. & Friedman, A. (2018). Can't Hurt Me: Master Your Mind and Defy the Odds. Lioncrest Publishing. / CNBC Make It (2019, May 15). How David Goggins Went From an Exterminator Living Paycheck-to-Paycheck to a Navy SEAL. cnbc.com. / Wikipedia: David Goggins. Born February 17, 1975, Buffalo, New York.

2 Goggins — recruiter calls, 297-pound weight requirement rejection, and two-week persistence: Goggins, D. & Friedman, A. (2018). Can't Hurt Me. / DVIDSHUB.net: The Toughest Man Alive: An Interview with Retired Navy SEAL David Goggins.

3 Goggins — training regimen, approximately 800–1,000 calories consumed daily, 106-pound loss in under three months: Goggins, D. & Friedman, A. (2018). Can't Hurt Me. / CNBC Make It (2019, May 15).

4 Goggins — BUD/S graduation Class 235, August 10, 2001; three Hell Week attempts (first: stress fractures and pneumonia; second: fractured kneecap; third: successful completion); Army Ranger School; Air Force TACP qualification. Pull-up record: 4,030 repetitions in 17 hours, 2013 Guinness World Record (subsequently surpassed). Sources: Wikipedia: David Goggins. / Military.com: Special Operations Profile: David Goggins.

5 Deliberate practice and competence development: Ericsson, K. A., Krampe, R. T., & Tesch-Römer, C. (1993). The Role of Deliberate Practice in the Acquisition of Expert Performance. Psychological Review, 100(3), 363–406.

6 Perfect conditions myth and delay-reinforcing behavior: Steel, P. (2007). The Nature of Procrastination: A Meta-Analytic and Theoretical Review of Quintessential Self-Regulatory Failure. Psychological Bulletin, 133(1), 65–94. Meta-analysis of more than 200 studies.

7 Confidence follows action — it does not precede it: Bandura, A. (1977). Self-Efficacy: Toward a Unifying Theory of Behavioral Change. Psychological Review, 84(2), 191–215. / Bandura, A. (1997). Self-Efficacy: The Exercise of Control. New York: W. H. Freeman.

8 Diminishing returns of passive preparation beyond a threshold: Brown, P. C., Roediger, H. L., & McDaniel, M. A. (2014). Make It Stick: The Science of Successful Learning. Cambridge, MA: Har-

vard University Press. / Ericsson, K. A. et al. (1993). The Role of Deliberate Practice.

9 Social accountability and commitment devices: Ariely, D. & Wertenbroch, K. (2002). Procrastination, Deadlines, and Performance: Self-Control by Precommitment. Psychological Science, 13(3), 219–224. / Gollwitzer, P. M. & Sheeran, P. (2006). Implementation Intentions and Goal Achievement: A Meta-Analysis of Effects and Processes. Advances in Experimental Social Psychology, 38, 69–119.

Epigraph note: The Benjamin Franklin quote ("Well done is better than well said.") is sourced from Poor Richard's Almanack (1737), confirmed via multiple Franklin scholarship sources.

CHAPTER 5 CITATIONS

1 Stephen King — biographical details including Hermon, Maine trailer, laundry room writing setup, Olivetti typewriter, $6,400 annual teaching salary, Tabitha's second-shift employment at Dunkin' Donuts: King, S. (2000). On Writing: A Memoir of the Craft. New York: Scribner. / Tabitha King's foreword to the 1991 Doubleday edition of Carrie (confirms trailer location in Hermon and laundry room setup). / Wikipedia: Carrie (novel). / Mental Floss (2024, April 5). How Stephen King's Wife Saved Carrie and Helped Launch His Career. mentalfloss.com. / Vincent, B. How Carrie Happened. stephenkingrevisited.com. Note: Some sources incorrectly place King in Bangor, Maine. Hermon is confirmed by King's own account in On Writing and Tabitha King's foreword.

2 King's 2,000-word daily target and ten-page daily goal: King, S. (2000). On Writing: A Memoir of the Craft. New York: Scribner.

King states: "I like to get ten pages a day, which amounts to 2,000 words."

3 Carrie — publishing history, advance, paperback rights, and King's share: Wikipedia: Carrie (novel). Doubleday advance of $2,500 confirmed. New American Library (Signet Books imprint) paperback rights of $400,000, King's contractual 50% share of $200,000, confirmed. Approximately 30 publisher rejections before Doubleday — range varies between 25 and 30 across sources; "approximately 30" is the appropriate qualifier. / Mental Floss (2024). / Vincent, B. How Carrie Happened. stephenkingrevisited.com.

4 Bandura, A. (2012). On the Functional Properties of Perceived Self-Efficacy Revisited. Journal of Management, 38(1), 9–44. Citing Collins, J. L. (1982). Self-Efficacy and Ability in Achievement Behavior. Paper presented at the American Educational Research Association; and Bouffard-Bouchard, T. (1990). Influence of Self-Efficacy on Performance in a Cognitive Task. Journal of Social Psychology, 130(3), 353–363. / Bandura, A. (1997). Self-Efficacy: The Exercise of Control. New York: W. H. Freeman. Note: Collins (1982) was a conference paper cited through Bandura's own later peer-reviewed work.

5 Linville, P. W. (1987). Self-complexity as a cognitive buffer against stress-related illness and depression. Journal of Personality and Social Psychology, 52(4), 663–676. Foundational study establishing self-complexity theory. People whose self-concept is organized around multiple distinct role-aspects are significantly more resistant to depression and stress than those organized around a single dominant identity. Widely cited across clinical, social, and organizational psychology for over three decades.

6 Stryker, S. (1968). Identity salience and role performance: The importance of symbolic interaction theory for family research. Journal of Marriage and the Family, 30, 558–564. Foundational paper establishing Identity Theory. Defines identity salience as the probability that a given identity will be invoked across situations and establishes the salience hierarchy as the primary organizational structure of the self-concept.

7 Stryker, S. & Serpe, R. T. (1982). Commitment, identity salience, and role behavior: Theory and research example. In W. Ickes & E. S. Knowles (Eds.), Personality, Roles, and Social Behavior. New York: Springer-Verlag. / Stryker, S. & Serpe, R. T. (1994). Identity salience and psychological centrality: Equivalent, overlapping, or complementary concepts? Social Psychology Quarterly, 57(1), 16–35. The 1982 paper establishes commitment — the density of social networks associated with a role — as the primary driver of identity salience. The 1994 paper establishes the critical distinction between identity salience (the probability of acting from an identity) and identity prominence (how much a person values an identity), demonstrating these are separate constructs that frequently do not align.

8 Manzi, C., Paderi, F., & Benet-Martínez, V. (2024). Multiple social identities and well-being: Insights from a person-centred approach. British Journal of Social Psychology, 63(2), 792–810. Study of 2,705 participants finding that high identification across multiple roles combined with strong identity integration — the perception that these identities work together coherently — is associated with the highest levels of psychological well-being. The configuration with low identification across roles and low integration was associated with the lowest well-being.

9 Brook, A. T., Garcia, J., & Fleming, M. A. (2008). The effects of multiple identities on psychological well-being. Personality and Social Psychology Bulletin, 34(12), 1588–1600. Key finding: when highly valued identities are in harmony — providing similar resources and expecting compatible behaviors — multiple identities increase well-being. When identities conflict and deplete resources, they decrease well-being.

10 Merolla, D. M., Serpe, R. T., Stryker, S., & Schultz, P. W. (2012). Structural precursors to identity processes: The role of proximate social structures. Social Psychology Quarterly, 75(2), 149–172. Study of 892 undergraduate students tracing the full causal chain: participation in role-relevant social structures increases commitment to an identity; commitment increases salience; salience increases behavioral intention and follow-through. External commitment is the mechanism that raises an identity from aspiration to operation.

Epigraph note: The William James quote ("Act as if what you do makes a difference. It does.") is confirmed in multiple James biographies and scholarly sources as representative of his documented views on will and habit. The precise wording varies slightly across transcribed sources.

CHAPTER 6 CITATIONS

1 Jocko Willink — 4:30 AM routine, "minimum requirements" quote, biographical details, and Michael Monsoor Medal of Honor: Wikipedia: Jocko Willink. / Business Insider (2017, November). A Retired Navy SEAL Commander Who Wakes Up at 4:30 AM Shares His Morning Routine. / Men's Journal (2025, June). Navy SEAL Shares the 2 Non-Negotiables That Anchor His Daily Rou-

tine. (Source of "minimum requirements" quote.) / CNBC Make It (2019, February). Ex-Navy SEAL Who Wakes Up at 4:30 AM: How to Get Out of Bed When You Don't Feel Like It. / Willink, J. & Babin, L. (2015). Extreme Ownership: How U.S. Navy SEALs Lead and Win. New York: St. Martin's Press. / Willink, J. (2017). Discipline Equals Freedom: Field Manual. New York: St. Martin's Press. Michael Monsoor Medal of Honor: awarded posthumously April 8, 2008, by President George W. Bush. Confirmed: Wikipedia: Michael Monsoor.

2 Dopamine habituation and novelty-based learning: Kutlu, M. G., Zachry, J., Melugin, P., et al. (2022). Dopamine Signaling in the Nucleus Accumbens Core Mediates Latent Inhibition. Nature Neuroscience. / Bromberg-Martin, E. S., Matsumoto, M., & Hikosaka, O. (2010). Dopamine in Motivational Control: Rewarding, Aversive, and Alerting. Neuron, 68(5), 815–834.

3 Discipline predicts academic success more powerfully than intelligence: Duckworth, A. L. & Seligman, M. E. P. (2005). Self-Discipline Outdoes IQ in Predicting Academic Performance of Adolescents. Psychological Science, 16(12), 939–944. Self-discipline accounted for more than twice the variance of IQ in final grades, school attendance, standardized test scores, and high school selection. / Duckworth, A. L., Peterson, C., Matthews, M. D., & Kelly, D. R. (2007). Grit: Perseverance and Passion for Long-Term Goals. Journal of Personality and Social Psychology, 92(6), 1087–1101. / Duckworth, A. L. (2016). Grit: The Power of Passion and Perseverance. New York: Scribner.

4 Habit formation and the 66-day average: Lally, P., van Jaarsveld, C. H. M., Potts, H. W. W., & Wardle, J. (2010). How Are Habits Formed: Modelling Habit Formation in the Real World. European

Journal of Social Psychology, 40(6), 998–1009. 96 participants, 12-week study. Time to automaticity ranged from 18 to 254 days; median 66 days. Missing one opportunity did not materially affect the habit formation process.

5 Progress monitoring and goal attainment: Harkin, B., Webb, T. L., Chang, B. P. I., et al. (2016). Does Monitoring Goal Progress Promote Goal Attainment? A Meta-Analysis of the Experimental Evidence. Psychological Bulletin, 142(2), 198–229. 138 studies, 19,951 participants.

6 Loss aversion: Kahneman, D. & Tversky, A. (1979). Prospect Theory: An Analysis of Decision Under Risk. Econometrica, 47(2), 263–291.

7 Chain method attribution: Isaac, B. (2007). Jerry Seinfeld's Productivity Secret. Lifehacker.com. / Seinfeld, J. Reddit AMA, 2014. Seinfeld noted the method was not his original idea. Attributed here to Isaac's 2007 popularization, with Seinfeld's public disclaimer noted.

Epigraph: Willink, J. (2017). Discipline Equals Freedom: Field Manual. New York: St. Martin's Press.

CHAPTER 7 CITATIONS

1 Paul MacCready, the Gossamer Condor, and the Kremer Prize: Wikipedia: Paul MacCready. / Wikipedia: Gossamer Condor. / Wikipedia: Kremer Prize. / Lemelson-MIT Program: Paul MacCready profile (lemelson.mit.edu). / National Inventors Hall of Fame: Paul B. MacCready. Verified facts: Kremer Prize established 1959 by Henry Kremer. Prize value: £50,000 (approximately

$100,000 USD at 1976 exchange rates). MacCready was the 1956 International Soaring Champion, the first American to win the title. PhD from Caltech. Construction began August 1976. Prize-winning flight: August 23, 1977, piloted by Bryan Allen at Minter Field, Shafter, California. Flight time: 7 minutes, 22 seconds. Materials: aluminum tubing, Mylar film, and piano wire. Wingspan: 96 feet.

2 One-way door / two-way door decision framework: Bezos, J. (2015). 2015 Letter to Amazon Shareholders. Amazon.com Investor Relations (ir.aboutamazon.com). Original passage: "Some decisions are consequential and irreversible or nearly irreversible — one-way doors — and these decisions must be made methodically, carefully, slowly, with great deliberation and consultation. But most decisions aren't like that — they are changeable, reversible — they're two-way doors."

3 Bezos 70% Rule and course-correction capacity: Bezos, J. (2016). 2016 Letter to Amazon Shareholders. Amazon.com Investor Relations (ir.aboutamazon.com). Full passage: "Most decisions should probably be made with somewhere around 70% of the information you wish you had. If you wait for 90%, in most cases, you're probably being slow. Plus, either way, you need to be good at quickly recognizing and correcting bad decisions. If you're good at course correcting, being wrong may be less costly than you think, whereas being slow is going to be expensive for sure."

4 Choice overload and decision paralysis: Iyengar, S. S. & Lepper, M. R. (2000). When Choice Is Demotivating: Can One Desire Too Much of a Good Thing? Journal of Personality and Social Psychology, 79(6), 995–1006. See Chapter 1 citation [4] for full study details. Conclusion directly applicable here: past a certain threshold,

additional information and options do not improve decisions — they prevent them.

5 Fast strategic decision-making and firm performance: Eisenhardt, K. M. (1989). Making Fast Strategic Decisions in High-Velocity Environments. Academy of Management Journal, 32(3), 543–576. Inductive study of eight microcomputer firms. Fast-deciding executive teams outperformed slow-deciding teams on all performance measures. Counterintuitively, fast decision-makers used more information and developed more alternatives, not fewer. Their advantage was in processing efficiently and acting before conditions changed.

Epigraph: Bezos, J. (2016). 2016 Letter to Amazon Shareholders. Amazon.com Investor Relations.

CHAPTER 8 CITATIONS

1 Antoni Gaudí and the Sagrada Família: Wikipedia: Sagrada Família. / Wikipedia: Antoni Gaudí. / Official Sagrada Família Foundation: sagradafamilia.org. Verified facts: Gaudí accepted the project in 1883 at age 31. He worked on it until his death on June 10, 1926, struck by a streetcar on June 7. One tower of the Nativity façade was completed at the time of his death. Construction passed the midpoint in 2010. Pope Benedict XVI consecrated the building November 7, 2010. The Sagrada Família became the tallest church in the world on October 30, 2025, at 162.91 meters. Construction of the central Tower of Jesus Christ is ongoing as of 2026. Total construction timeline: 144 years and counting. The "My client is not in a hurry" quote is widely attributed to Gaudí across multiple biographical sources; primary source documentation varies. Presented as reported speech.

2 Warren Buffett — compound wealth timeline: Schroeder, A. (2008). The Snowball: Warren Buffett and the Business of Life. New York: Bantam Books. / Hagstrom, R. G. (2014). The Warren Buffett Way. Hoboken, NJ: Wiley. Buffett began investing at age 11. Became a billionaire at approximately age 56. The 95 percent figure reflects the proportion of net worth accumulated after age 65 relative to total lifetime net worth, a widely documented characteristic of compound returns at scale confirmed across multiple financial biographies.

3 Planning fallacy: Kahneman, D. & Tversky, A. (1979). Intuitive prediction: Biases and corrective procedures. In S. Makridakis & S. C. Wheelwright (Eds.), TIMS Studies in Management Science, 12, 313–327. / Kahneman, D. (2011). Thinking, Fast and Slow. New York: Farrar, Straus and Giroux. The planning fallacy describes the systematic tendency to underestimate time, costs, and risks of future actions while overestimating their benefits. Confirmed across organizational, individual, and governmental planning contexts.

4 Fitts, P. M. & Posner, M. I. (1967). Human Performance. Belmont, CA: Brooks/Cole. The three-stage skill acquisition model — cognitive, associative, and autonomous — is one of the most widely cited frameworks in cognitive and motor learning science. Progress plateaus between stages even as neurological adaptation continues underneath.

5 Seed germination and radicle-first development sequence: Campbell, N. A. & Reece, J. B. (2005). Biology (7th ed.). San Francisco: Benjamin Cummings.

6 Hurricane formation and tropical development stages: National Hurricane Center, NOAA. nhc.noaa.gov. The four-stage tropical

development classification (tropical disturbance, tropical depression, tropical storm, hurricane) and the energy accumulation timeline are documented in NOAA's official hurricane formation explanations.

Epigraph: Tolstoy, L. (1869). War and Peace. Book 10, Chapter 16.

CHAPTER 9 CITATIONS

1 WD-40 — origin, development history, and naming: WD-40 Company official history (wd40.com). / Wikipedia: WD-40. / Snopes.com fact-check: What Does WD-40 Stand For (confirmed true). Formula developed 1953 by the Rocket Chemical Company, San Diego, California. Name: Water Displacement, 40th formula, per official company history. Formula never patented to protect the secrecy of the formulation. First commercial sale: 1958.

Epigraph: Dillard, A. (1989). The Writing Life. New York: Harper & Row.

CHAPTER 10 CITATIONS

1 Jim Collins — flywheel concept and Good to Great research: Collins, J. (2001). Good to Great: Why Some Companies Make the Leap and Others Don't. New York: HarperBusiness. / Collins, J. (2019). Turning the Flywheel: A Monograph to Accompany Good to Great. New York: HarperBusiness. Flywheel description (5,000-pound disk, 30-foot diameter): jimcollins.com/concepts/the-flywheel.html.

2 Amazon virtuous cycle — napkin sketch origin and first annual profit: Stone, B. (2013). The Everything Store: Jeff Bezos and the

Age of Amazon. New York: Little, Brown and Company. The precise circumstances of the napkin sketch vary slightly across secondary sources. Amazon first full-year profitability: Amazon 2003 Annual Report. Amazon founded 1994.

3 Yvon Chouinard and the founding of Patagonia: Chouinard, Y. (2005). Let My People Go Surfing: The Education of a Reluctant Businessman. New York: Penguin Press. / Patagonia official company history: patagonia.com/company-history. / Wikipedia: Yvon Chouinard. / 1972 Chouinard Equipment catalog, including Doug Robinson's 14-page essay "The Whole Natural Art of Protection" and the Chouinard-Frost editorial on clean climbing: archived at ClimbAZ.com and The Seneca Project. Pitons at 70% of revenue: confirmed in Chouinard (2005), Wikipedia, and multiple climbing history sources. Forge purchased 1957; partnership with Tom Frost 1965; Chouinard Equipment largest U.S. climbing hardware supplier by 1970: Patagonia company history. Rugby shirts purchased in Scotland 1970; Patagonia founded 1973: Patagonia company history and Chouinard (2005). Ownership transferred to the Patagonia Purpose Trust and Holdfast Collective in September 2022: Patagonia official announcement.

4 Pets.com: Wikipedia: Pets.com. / IPO: February 11, 2000, at $11 per share. / Closure announced: November 7, 2000. / Operating as a public company: 268 days. / Total funding raised: over $300 million per contemporaneous reporting. / Coulter, M. & Vogel, K. C. (2004). Pets.com: A Dot-com Failure. Issues in Accounting Education.

Epigraph: Collins, J. (2019). Turning the Flywheel. New York: HarperBusiness.

CHAPTER 11 CITATIONS

1 Bill Walsh — "The score takes care of itself": Walsh, B., Jamison, S., & Walsh, C. (2009). The Score Takes Care of Itself: My Philosophy of Leadership. New York: Portfolio/Penguin. Published posthumously; Walsh died July 30, 2007. The title phrase is documented in the book and in multiple primary Walsh interviews conducted before his death.

2 Flywheel integration and failure modes: See Chapter 10 citations. Collins, J. (2001). Good to Great. New York: HarperBusiness. / Collins, J. (2019). Turning the Flywheel. New York: HarperBusiness.

3 Jocko Willink — 4:30 AM discipline routine: Willink, J. & Babin, L. (2015). Extreme Ownership: How U.S. Navy SEALs Lead and Win. New York: St. Martin's Press. / Willink, J. (2017). Discipline Equals Freedom: Field Manual. New York: St. Martin's Press. Self-reported consistently across public content including the Jocko Podcast.

4 Dopamine normalization and habit formation timeline: Lally, P., van Jaarsveld, C. H. M., Potts, H. W. W., & Wardle, J. (2010). How Are Habits Formed: Modelling Habit Formation in the Real World. European Journal of Social Psychology, 40(6), 998–1009.

5 Commitment devices and consequences: Ariely, D. & Wertenbroch, K. (2002). Procrastination, Deadlines, and Performance: Self-Control by Precommitment. Psychological Science, 13(3), 219–224. Pre-committing a specific, uncomfortable consequence for breaking a commitment significantly increases follow-through.

Epigraph: Walsh, B., Jamison, S., & Walsh, C. (2009). The Score Takes Care of Itself. New York: Portfolio/Penguin.

CONCLUSION CITATIONS

1 Diogenes the Cynic and the motion debate — source of *solvitur ambulando*: The account of Diogenes silently rising and walking in response to a philosophical argument against the existence of motion originates in Simplicius of Cilicia, *Commentary on Aristotle's Physics* (c. 530 AD), in his discussion of Zeno's paradoxes. Simplicius of Cilicia (c. 480 – c. 540 AD) was a Neoplatonist philosopher whose commentaries on Aristotle's works are the primary surviving source for numerous fragments of earlier Greek philosophy. His *Commentary on Aristotle's Physics* (In Aristotelis Physicorum libros) is edited in Commentaria in Aristotelem Graeca (CAG), Hermann Diels, ed., 2 vols., Berlin: Reimer, 1882–1895. The Diogenes anecdote and its connection to the phrase *solvitur ambulando* are confirmed in: Huggett, Nick, "Zeno's Paradoxes," *The Stanford Encyclopedia of Philosophy* (Fall 2024 Edition), Edward N. Zalta & Uri Nodelman, eds., plato.stanford.edu. / Wikipedia: Solvitur ambulando (citing the Simplicius source).

2 Zeno of Elea and the paradoxes of motion: Zeno of Elea (c. 490–430 BCE) formulated several paradoxes of motion — including the Dichotomy, Achilles and the Tortoise, and the Arrow — to defend the Eleatic position that motion and change are illusory. The paradoxes survive primarily through Aristotle's *Physics* (Books VI and VIII) and through Simplicius's commentary on the same. The standard scholarly reference is: Huggett, Nick, "Zeno's Paradoxes," *The Stanford Encyclopedia of Philosophy* (Fall 2024 Edition), plato.stanford.edu. For primary text: Aristotle, *Physics*, Books

VI–VIII, in *The Complete Works of Aristotle*, Jonathan Barnes, ed. Princeton: Princeton University Press, 1984.

3 *Solvitur ambulando* — attribution and usage history: The Latin phrase *solvitur ambulando* ("it is solved by walking") is widely attributed to Saint Augustine in later tradition but originates in the Diogenes anecdote recorded by Simplicius. It has been invoked by writers across centuries as shorthand for the principle that practical demonstration supersedes abstract argument. Notable documented uses include: Lewis Carroll, "What the Tortoise Said to Achilles," *Mind*, Vol. 4, No. 14 (1895), pp. 278–280 (the phrase appears in Carroll's retelling of the Zeno debate); Douglas Hofstadter, *Gödel, Escher, Bach: An Eternal Golden Braid*, New York: Basic Books, 1979, ISBN 0-465-02656-7 (Hofstadter references the Diogenes anecdote in his discussion of paradox and self-reference); Bruce Chatwin, *The Songlines*, London: Jonathan Cape, 1986 (cited in Patrick Leigh Fermor: An Adventure, Artemis Cooper, 2012, p. 373, ISBN 978-0-7195-5449-0). Etymology confirmed: Harper, Douglas, "Etymology of *solvitur ambulando*," *Online Etymology Dictionary*, etymonline.com.

4 Diogenes the Cynic — biographical background: Diogenes of Sinope (c. 412–323 BCE), known as Diogenes the Cynic, was a Greek philosopher and one of the founders of Cynicism. He was born in Sinope (modern Sinop, Turkey), exiled to Athens, and is documented in Diogenes Laërtius, *Lives of the Eminent Philosophers*, Book VI. Standard scholarly reference: Long, A. A., "The Socratic Tradition: Diogenes, Crates, and Hellenistic Ethics," in *The Cambridge Companion to the Stoics*, Brad Inwood, ed., Cambridge: Cambridge University Press, 2003. / Wikipedia: Diogenes the Cynic.

Note on attribution: Solvitur ambulando is often attributed to Saint Augustine in popular sources. The original account, Diogenes of Sinope rising and walking in response to Zeno's argument against motion, is recorded by Simplicius of Cilicia in his Commentary on Aristotle's Physics (c. 530 AD) and is the academically supported primary source for the phrase.

ABOUT THE AUTHOR

Ryan Grimes is an entrepreneur, author, and business consultant specializing in operational efficiency optimization. Before writing Execute First, Ryan spent 5 years serving in the United States Marine Corps and over 20 years as a business leader and entrepreneur. His passion for uncovering the patterns, characteristics and habits that are responsible for what makes some people successful, and what keeps others from ever finding success, led him to the contents of this book. His extensive experience forms the knowledge base of his writing, consulting and speaking where he shares the tools he has discovered, so anyone can achieve higher levels of success. Ryan's work has made him an expert in the field of business and personal development. Today, Ryan helps entrepreneurs and elite performers bridge the gap between knowing and doing through an emphasis on focused systematic execution.

Execute First

Ryan Grimes

HENSLEY
PRESS